BEN FRANKLIN
INVENTING AMERICA

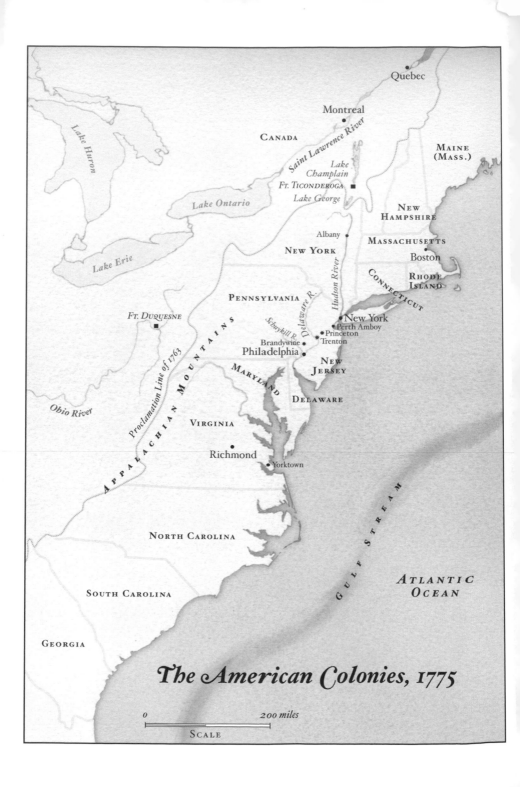

The American Colonies, 1775

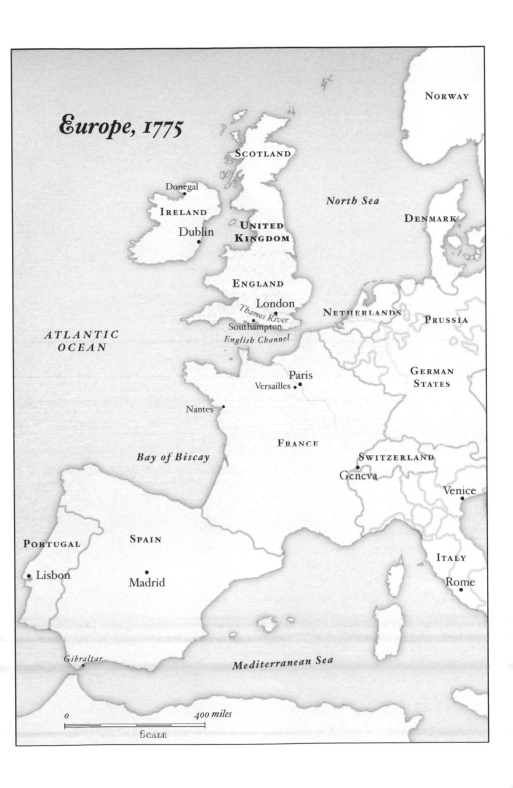

Benjamin Franklin

BEN FRANKLIN
INVENTING AMERICA

THOMAS FLEMING

STERLING PUBLISHING CO., INC.
New York

A FLYING POINT PRESS BOOK

Design: PlutoMedia
Front cover painting: Michael Deas
Frontispiece: The Granger Collection, New York

Library of Congress Cataloging-in-Publication Data

Fleming, Thomas J.
Benjamin Franklin : inventing America / Thomas Fleming. — Updated ed.
p. cm. — (Sterling point books)
Includes index.
ISBN-13: 978-1-4027-4523-2 (trade)
ISBN-10: 1-4027-4523-0 (trade)
ISBN-13: 978-1-4027-4143-2 (paper)
ISBN-10: 1-4027-4143-X (paper)
1. Franklin, Benjamin, 1706-1790—Juvenile literature. 2. Statesmen—United States—Biography—
Juvenile literature. 3. Inventors—United States—Biography—
Juvenile literature. 4. Scientists—United States—Biography—Juvenile literature.
5. Printers—United States—Biography—Juvenile literature. I. Title.

E302.6.F8F565 2007
973.3092—dc22
[B]
2006032142

2   4   6   8   10   9   7   5   3   1

Published by Sterling Publishing Co., Inc.
387 Park Avenue South, New York, NY 10016
Original edition published by Four Winds Press
Copyright © 1973 by Thomas J. Fleming
New material in this updated edition
Copyright © 2007 by Flying Point Press
Maps copyright © by Richard Thompson, Creative Freelancers, Inc.
Distributed in Canada by Sterling Publishing
c/o Canadian Manda Group, 165 Dufferin Street
Toronto, Ontario, Canada M6K 3H6
Distributed in the United Kingdom by GMC Distribution Services
Castle Place, 166 High Street, Lewes, East Sussex, England BN7 1XU
Distributed in Australia by Capricorn Link (Australia) Pty. Ltd.
P.O. Box 704, Windsor, NSW 2756, Australia

Sterling ISBN-13: 978-1-4027-4143-2
ISBN-10: 1-4027-4143-X

For information about custom editions, special sales, premium and
corporate purchases, please contact Sterling Special Sales Department at
800-805-5489 or specialsales@sterlingpub.com.

CONTENTS

CONTENTS

BEN FRANKLIN
INVENTING AMERICA

CHAPTER 1

THE APPRENTICE

ONE DAY IN 1771, WHILE VISITING FRIENDS IN the village of Twyford, not far from Southampton in southwestern England, Benjamin Franklin decided to write a letter to his son William. He sat down in the red brick summerhouse in the garden, with the door open and the August sunshine streaming in. "Dear Son," he began. The letter became famous because it grew over the next three weeks into a book. In this book, Franklin told his son many things William did not know about his father's boyhood in Boston.

"I do not remember when I could not read," Benjamin told his son. His father, Josiah, had decided that Benjamin's fondness for books meant he would make a good minister. Josiah sent Ben to the local grammar school where, in one year, he rose to the head of the class, and then skipped into the class above it.

But Ben's father had a big family—four children by his first wife and ten by his second wife. "I remember thirteen sitting at one time at his table," Benjamin wrote. He was the youngest son, but there were two younger daughters. Josiah Franklin decided he could not afford to send his son all the way through grammar school and college, and sent him to another school where the instruction was limited to writing and arithmetic. Benjamin very quickly learned to write, but he failed in arithmetic.

When Benjamin was ten, Josiah Franklin brought the boy home to work for him in his candle- and soap-making business. Ben cut wicks for the candles, filled the dipping mold, worked behind the counter in the shop where the candles and soap were sold, and ran errands for his father. Soon he had seen enough to know he "disliked the trade."

"What do you want to do?" his father asked. "Go to sea," replied Ben. This upset his father very much, for an older son, Josiah, had become a sailor and then drowned when his ship sank. His father tred to persuade young Benjamin to choose another trade, taking the boy for walks with him around Boston to let him watch bricklayers, carpenters and other tradesmen at work. Though Ben was fascinated by the skill with which these men handled their tools and learned how to use many of them himself, he did not find a trade that interested him.

Meanwhile, he enjoyed himself. Boston was surrounded by water and Ben had learned to swim almost as soon as he could walk. Like most children, he wanted to swim as fast as possible, and one day he decided to improve on his natural equipment. "I made two oval palettes, each about ten inches long and six broad, with a hole for the thumb, in order to retain it fast in the palm of my hand. They much resembled a painter's palettes. In swimming I pushed the edges of these forward, and I struck the water with their flat surfaces and I drew them back . . . I swam faster by means of these palettes, but they fatigued my wrists. I also fitted to the soles of my feet a kind of sandals; but I was not satisfied with them because I observed that the stroke is partly given by the inside of the feet and the ankles, and not entirely with the soles of the feet. . . ."

Then one day, while flying a paper kite near the bank of a big pond—nearly a mile wide—Ben got an even better idea. The water suddenly looked too good to resist, so Ben tied the string of the kite to a stake, tore off his clothes, and jumped into the pond. The kite continued to fly, and Ben decided to enjoy flying the kite and swimming at the same time. He climbed out of the water, seized the kite string and then jumped back in. Flipping over on his back, he held the string in his hands, and the kite continued to soar. Suddenly he noticed that the kite had become a sail, and he called to one of his friends on the bank of the pond and told him to carry his clothes over to the other side. "My kite . . . carried me quite over without the least fatigue and with the greatest pleasure imaginable," he wrote. "I was only obliged occasionally to halt a little in my course, and resist its progress, when it

3

appeared that by following too quick I lowered the kite too much."

Among friends his own age, Ben was always the leader. In a boat or canoe, he gave the orders, "especially in any case of difficulty," though sometimes, he admitted, he led his friends into "scrapes." One of their pastimes was fishing for minnows on the edge of the pond, where the land was marshy. It often became "a mere quagmire" into which they sank, muddying their clothes. One day Ben decided they needed a wharf. Looking around, he saw "a large heap of stones which were intended for a new house near the marsh, and which would very well suit our purpose." In the evening, after the builders departed, Ben assembled a group of his friends, and, working "like so many ants," they lugged the stones down to the marsh and built their "little wharf." The next morning, the workmen were very annoyed to discover the stones missing, but they soon found out who had taken them. Benjamin's father gave his son a severe lecture, reminding him, against the boy's pleas about "the usefulness of the work," that "nothing was useful which was not honest." Benjamin loved and respected his father, and he never forgot that advice.

By the time Josiah Franklin had decided on a trade for Benjamin, James Franklin, Benjamin's older brother, was already in business as a printer in Boston. Printing seemed a very logical business for someone as interested in words as Benjamin, who continued to read every book he could find, even spending his own money on books. So at the age of twelve, Benjamin was "bound" as an apprentice to his older brother by an agreement which stipulated that he would have to remain an apprentice until he was twenty-one. Benjamin quickly learned how to set type and operate a printing press, but in his spare time he continued to read every book he could buy or borrow. "Often I sat up in my room reading the greatest part of the night," he said.

Benjamin soon decided that he wanted to become a writer. He was inclined to poetry, and wrote some "little pieces" which he showed his brother James, who urged him to compose some ballads. He wrote two, "The Lighthouse Tragedy," about the drowning of a ship's captain and his two daughters, and "A Sailor's Song" about the capture of Blackbeard the pirate. James printed these ballads and sent Benjamin around Boston to sell them. "The Lighthouse Tragedy" sold "wonderfully" because it was about a recent event. Benjamin was enormously flattered; he thought he was on his way to becoming a famous poet. Then Josiah Franklin took him aside for a father-to-son talk. He told Ben that his poetry was very poor stuff. Moreover, it was no profession for anyone born poor, for versemakers were generally beggars. Instead, he encouraged Benjamin to learn how to write good prose.

Around this time, Benjamin became friendly with another young Bostonian named John Collins, who was also a great reader. The boys were fond of arguing; sometimes they put their arguments into writing. Josiah Franklin pointed out that Ben's writing was far inferior to Collins', and Ben realizing he was right, thereafter grew more attentive to "the manner" in writing and worked daily to improve himself. He found a volume of *The Spectator,* the famous English newspaper written by Joseph Addison and Richard Steele, and thought "the writing excellent." After he read one of the essays, he made notes on each sentence and then would put them aside for a few days. Then, without referring to *The Spectator,* he tried to rewrite his notes and compared the result to the original essay. This helped him correct some of his faults, but he found his biggest problem was his limited vocabulary. Ben tried to solve this problem by turning *The Spectator* essays into rhyme. In order to "suit the measure" or find a different sound for a rhyme, he was constantly forced to use new words, thereby enlarging his vocabulary. Next he took all his notes and jumbled them together, and then tried to "reduce them into the best order" to teach himself "method in the arrangement of thoughts." Again, he compared his work to the original essay in *The Spectator,* and criticized the results.

While struggling to improve himself as a writer, Benjamin did not neglect his other talents. He was ashamed of his failure to learn arithmetic, and on his own he bought a textbook and taught himself all that he needed to know in that field. At the same time he acquired another skill. After reading "Memorable Things of Socrates," by the Greek historian Xenophon, Benjamin decided he liked Socrates' way of arguing by asking questions. Dropping his habit of "abrupt contradiction and positive argumentation" and instead pretending to be a "humble enquirer and doubter," Ben soon became "very artful and expert in drawing people even of superior knowledge into . . . difficulties out of which they could not extricate themselves." Often, he admitted, he obtained victories "that neither my self nor my cause deserved."

Meanwhile, James Franklin had begun to publish a newspaper, *The New England Courant*. Along with printing the news, James had the clever idea of asking his friends to write amusing little essays for the paper. These writings made it more popular, and Benjamin decided he would like to get into the act. Although he was only a boy, Ben already sensed that his brother was jealous of his skill as a writer. So Ben carefully disguised his handwriting, wrote an unsigned essay and slipped it under the door of the printing house one night. James Franklin showed the essay to his writing friends; and while young Benjamin worked away at his typesetting, he listened with "exquisite pleasure" while the older men praised the quality of the writing and tried to guess who was the author.

The name Franklin had signed to the bottom of the letter was "Silence Dogood." He pretended to be the widow of a country minister, and commented on the manners and morals of New England. Harvard College came in for some very sharp comments in Mrs. Dogood's fourth essay. Noting that most parents consulted only their purses instead of their children's capacities in deciding whether to send their children to this "temple of learning," she observed that, as a result, at graduation "every beetle-scull seem'd well satisfy'd with his own portion of learning, tho' perhaps he was e'en just as ignorant as ever." [After graduation, what happened?] "Some . . . took to merchandising, others to traveling, some to one thing, some to another, and some to nothing; and many of them . . . liv'd as poor as churchmice, being unable to dig, and asham'd to beg, and to live by their wits it was impossible." No wonder so many of them became ministers, Mrs. Dogood concluded. All they had learned at Harvard was how to "carry themselves hand-somely, and enter a room genteely (which might as well be acquir'd at a dancing school)." She ended her essay by urging parents not to be so "blind to their children's dulness, and insensible of the solidity of their sculls."

Mrs. Dogood contributed fourteen essays to *The New England Courant,* and then her creator, Benjamin Franklin, triumphantly revealed his identity to his brother and his friends. James Franklin was not pleased; he became even more jealous of Benjamin. The two brothers were soon quar-reling constantly, and taking their disputes to their father for settlement. Josiah Franklin tended to favor Benjamin, so James decided to settle future arguments with his fists. Ben-jamin took these beatings "extreamly amiss" and soon found himself "continually wishing" for a chance to shorten his apprenticeship.

CHAPTER 2

THE RUNAWAY

BENJAMIN'S OPPORTUNITY TO LEAVE HIS BROTHER arrived a few months later, when James Franklin criticized the Massachusetts Assembly and was imprisoned for a month. Freedom of the press as we now know it in America and other democratic nations did not exist in those days. While his brother was in jail, Benjamin ran the *Courant*. The Assembly finally released James Franklin, but they ordered him to stop printing his paper. To circumvent this oppressive ruling, James transferred the ownership of the paper to Ben. To make this maneuver legal he had to release Benjamin from his apprenticeship. Secretly, he had Benjamin sign a new "indenture," as the terms of an apprenticeship were called.

Within a matter of months, a new argument erupted between the brothers and James once more resorted to his fists. Angrily, Benjamin informed his brother that he considered himself a free man and was quitting his job. He knew that James would not dare to enforce the secret indenture that he had signed. In a resentful fury, James Franklin did the next worse thing and went to every printer in Boston, warning them not to give Benjamin any work. His father disapproved of Benjamin's decision, and since he was only seventeen his family could legally force him to stay in Boston. So he decided to run away.

Benjamin's friend Collins arranged for his passage to New York on a sloop and Benjamin sold some of his books to raise a little money. In three days he was in New York, "near three hundred miles from home . . . without the least recommendation to or knowledge of any person in the place." There was no work for printers in New York, and Benjamin struggled on to Philadelphia.

The trip turned into a miserable ordeal. Stormy weather harassed the boat that took him from New York to Perth Amboy, turning a journey of two or three hours into thirty hours without food or water. The runaway trudged across central New Jersey on foot, through soaking rain, and finally arrived in Philadelphia at 9 o'clock on Sunday morning, filthy and exhausted. He bought some bread and wandered around town eating it, then went to church with some Quakers and fell asleep in the middle of their service. A friendly Quaker took him to the Crooked Billet Tavern on Water Street, where Ben rented a room and slept most of the day and all of the night. The next morning he cleaned himself up and went looking for work.

All Benjamin could find was part-time work with a weird character named Keimer, whose printing equipment consisted of "an old shatter'd press" and one small worn-out font of English type. Keimer had a full-length beard, long hair and wore dirty tattered clothes, and, to complete the picture of an eccentric, he lived in a house with no furniture.

Keimer loved to argue about religion, but he found young Ben too much for him. "I us'd to work him so with my Socratic method," Ben said, "and trepann'd him so often by questions apparently so distant from any point we had in hand and yet by degrees led to the point . . . that at last he grew ridiculously cautious and would hardly answer me the most common question without asking first, *What do you intend to infer from that?*" Keimer was so impressed with Ben as a disputer that he asked him to join in establishing a new religion. Keimer would preach the doctrines, and Ben would refute all the opponents.

Meanwhile, they found very little printing to do. With funds running low, Ben suggested they become vegetarians. He had experimented with this kind of diet before he left Boston, and knew he could put up with it. But Keimer was "a great glutton" and he found the diet almost unendurable, in spite of a list of forty dishes which Ben had a neighborhood woman prepare for them at different times. Finally, Keimer could stand the vegetarian meals no longer, and ordered a roast pig. He invited

Ben and two women friends to dine with him, but the neighborhood cook brought the pig before the guests arrived. Keimer, Ben said, "could not resist the temptation" and ate the whole pig before they came.

Ben's adventures with Keimer were interrupted by the appearance of his brother-in-law Robert Holmes, captain of a sloop that traded between Boston and Delaware. Holmes had heard that Ben was in Philadelphia and wrote him a letter, urging him to return to Boston. Ben replied by mail, and Holmes showed his letter to Sir William Keith, the Governor of Pennsylvania, hoping that he would urge the runaway to go home. Instead, Keith declared himself most impressed by Ben's skill as a writer, and announced that he wanted to set him up as a printer in Philadelphia. Keith went to Keimer's shop and conversed with Ben "in a most affable, friendly and familiar manner imaginable." The Governor invited the young man to his home for dinner, and explained what he had in mind. Ben was naturally delighted, and he soon went back to Boston with a letter in his pocket from Governor Keith, urging his father to loan him the money he needed to set up a printing shop.

Josiah Franklin read the Governor's letter, but "said little of it" to Ben for some days. When Captain Holmes returned, Josiah asked him what he thought of Keith. Holmes did his best to give a favorable impression, but Josiah finally spoke his mind: The Governor must be a man of "small discretion" to think of setting an eighteen-year-old boy up in business. To

Ben's chagrin, Josiah wrote a polite letter to Keith, thanking him for the offer, but declining to risk the money. The cost of equipping a small print shop was a hundred pounds—the modern day equivalent being $14,000.

Ben's brother James refused to hire him again, so Josiah gave his son permission to return to Philadelphia. He urged Ben to "avoid lampooning in the Silence Dogood style," work hard and save his money. By the time he was twenty-one, he ought to have nearly enough money to set himself up in business and if he "came near the matter" Josiah would give him the rest.

Ben's friend John Collins decided to return to Philadelphia with him. Ben went overland to New York and met Collins there. To Ben's amazement he discovered his friend had acquired a great fondness for brandy and had been drunk every day since his arrival in New York. Collins had lost his money gambling, and Ben had to pay the bill at his boarding house and put up money for the rest of the journey to Philadelphia. There, Collins had trouble finding work, and continued to drink and live off Ben. Liquor made him belligerent, and the friends almost always quarreled when Collins drank.

One night while rowing in a boat on the Delaware, their friendship came to an end. There were several other young men in the boat, and each had taken a turn at the oars. But Collins had been drinking, and he suddenly announced, "I will be rowed home."

"We will not row you," Ben said.

"You must or stay all night on the water," Collins said.

The others were inclined to give up the argument. "Let us row him," they said. But Ben refused. Collins became more and more ugly tempered, finally swearing he would make Ben row or throw him overboard. Collins lurched to his feet and came toward Ben, swinging his fists. Ben grabbed Collins by the seat of the pants and threw him head first into the river.

Collins was a good swimmer, so he was in no danger of drowning. But before he could reach the boat, Ben ordered his fellow oarsmen to put it out of his reach. Every time Collins came close to the boat, they asked him if he would row. "No," he would cry and they would pull away from him again. "He was ready to die with vexation," Ben reported. But Collins obstinately refused to row. Finally he began to tire, and Ben dragged him into the boat "and brought him home dripping wet in the evening.

"We hardly exchanged a civil word afterwards," Ben said. A few weeks later Collins went to the West Indies as a tutor for the sons of a wealthy planter there. He promised to pay back Ben the money he owed him. "But I never heard of him after," Ben said.

Meanwhile, Governor Keith remained determined to set Ben up as a printer. "Give me an inventory of the things necessary to be had from England," he said, "and I will send for them. You shall repay me when you are able."

Ben did not have "the least doubt of his meaning what he said," and he gave the Governor an inventory of what he needed. But then Keith had another idea. Why didn't Ben go to England and choose the types and other equipment personally? He might also be able to make arrangements with booksellers and stationers to import and sell their books and paper. The offer was irresistible to an adventurous young man. An opportunity to see London, capital of the British Empire, to an American colonist the greatest city in the world! Ben eagerly accepted, and thereby made one of his first serious mistakes, or, as he called them in printers' language, "errata."

For some time he had been seeing a young girl his own age—Deborah Read, the daughter of a Philadelphia shopkeeper. They were in love and already talking about marriage. But the prospect of going on a long voyage made Ben decide to put off marriage until his return from England. So he left poor Deborah, obviously heartbroken, behind him and sailed for England. In the ship's mailbag, Governor Keith assured him, were numerous letters of recommendation from him to important men in England, which would enable Ben to buy all the equipment he needed, on the Governor's credit.

After a long, stormy voyage, the ship finally reached London on the 24th of December, 1724. The Captain opened the mailbag and Ben was puzzled to discover no letters with his name on them. But he picked out several that seemed to be in the Governor's handwriting. He trudged into the city from the Thames River docks and presented his first letter to a stationer. The man opened it and said, "Oh, Riddlesden; I have lately found him to be a complete rascal and I will have nothing to do with him nor receive any letters from him." He handed the letter back to Ben and turned to wait on a customer.

Ben swiftly discovered that none of the letters were from Governor Keith. Baffled, he sought out a friend he had made on the voyage, a Philadelphia merchant named Thomas Denham. Haltingly, Ben explained why he was in London. (He had kept the purpose of his trip a secret at the Governor's advice.) Denham laughed heartily at the idea that Governor Keith could give Ben a letter of credit to buy equipment. He had, said Denham, "no credit to give." Why had the Governor played such a trick on a poor ignorant boy? It was, Mr. Denham explained, a habit he had acquired. "He wished to please everybody, and having little to give, he gave expectations."

"What should I do?" Ben asked in bewilderment. He was 3,000 miles from home, without a cent in his pocket.

CHAPTER 3

THE SWIMMING INSTRUCTOR

THERE WAS ONLY ONE THING TO DO—BEN WENT to work as a printer. To his delight, he found he was easily the equal of English printers. In fact, he could work harder and longer than most of them. By now Ben was a husky eighteen-year-old, almost six feet tall with extremely muscular arms and shoulders. While most printers needed both hands to carry one large form of type up and down stairs, Ben carried a form in each hand. The master printer, noting his quickness at composing, gave Ben all the work which required speed. He thus made more money than his fellow journeymen.

Ben tried to save his money, but he had a problem similar to the one Collins had given him in Philadelphia. Another friend, James Ralph, who had made the voyage with him, wanted to become a poet or a playwright. But he found it very difficult to get any work at all, and so he lived off Ben's earnings.

17

Although Ralph had a wife in Philadelphia, he fell in love with a young woman who ran a millinery shop. They lived together as man and wife, and she lost her friends and her business. Ben was soon supporting both of them. In desperation, Ralph took a teaching job in the country. His English "wife" continued to visit Ben, who found himself falling in love with her. When Ben suggested that he take Ralph's place, the lady angrily rejected him, and informed Ralph, who rushed back to London, denounced Ben and grandly informed him that he considered all his debts canceled. By now these amounted to some 27 pounds, no small sum at the time. (In today's money it was about $2,700 of purchasing power.)

Thereafter, Ben struggled mightily to save every possible cent to pay for his voyage back to Philadelphia. Saving this money was a long, slow struggle, lasting almost two years. Without Ralph's company he was lonely and homesick.

Toward the end of this period, Ben almost gave up printing and opened a swimming school. He had become friendly with another young printer, who had received a good education and read Latin and spoke French. Ben taught him and a friend how to swim in only two visits to the Thames.

One day, on a trip down the river with this young man and a number of his other friends, the young printer began telling everyone what a remarkable swimmer Ben Franklin was. Although England was a seafaring nation, few people could swim, and everyone became very curious to see Ben perform. Agreeably, he stripped off most of his clothes, leaped into the

Thames and swam from Chelsea to Blackfriar's—a distance of about three and a half miles. He dove like a porpoise, floated on his back, and swam under water, all of which "surpriz'd and pleas'd those to whom they were novelties."

A wealthy Englishman heard about this performance, and asked Ben to call on him. His sons were preparing to leave on a tour of Europe, he explained, and he would like them to be taught swimming. The sum of money he offered Ben made the young man's head spin, and Ben suddenly realized that he could make a great deal of money teaching Englishmen how to swim. But reluctantly he gave up the idea, and told his wealthy customer that he could not teach his sons. Ben was going back to America.

Thomas Denham, the merchant who had told Ben the truth about Governor Keith, had kept in touch with his young friend over the past year and a half. Now he offered to take Ben back to Philadelphia with him, and give him a job as his clerk in a store he planned to open there. Ben had accepted the offer, before the idea of a swimming school had occurred to him. Perhaps he would have accepted Denham's offer anyway. "I was grown tired of London," he said, "remember'd with pleasure the happy months I had spent in Pennsylvania, and wish'd again to see it."

On the long voyage back to Philadelphia, Ben kept a journal. In it he described the various English towns they passed while going down the Channel, and once on the ocean, the weather, the fish they caught, and the characters of his fellow voyagers.

For the first time he revealed one of the talents that was to make him famous—the keen, observing eye of a scientist.

"This afternoon we took up several branches of gulfweed," he wrote on September 28th, 1726. Gulfweed was the vegetation which grew in the Gulf Stream, the great ocean river that runs from the Gulf of Mexico across the Atlantic.

One of these branches had something peculiar in it. In common with the rest, it had a leaf about three-quarters of an inch long, indented like a saw, and a small yellow berry, filled with nothing but wind; besides which it bore a fruit of the animal kind, very surprising to see. It was a small shellfish like a heart, the stalk by which it proceeded from the branch being partly of a grizzly kind. Upon this one branch of the weed, there were near forty of these vegetable animals; the smallest of them, near the end, contained a substance somewhat like an oyster, but the larger were visibly animated, opening their shells every moment, and thrusting out a set of unformed claws, not unlike those of a crab; but the inner part was still a kind of soft jelly. Observing the weed more narrowly, I spied a very small crab crawling along it, about as big as the head of a tenpenny nail, and of a yellowish color, like the weed itself. This gave me some reason to think that he was a native of the branch; that he had not long since been in the same condition with the rest of those little embryos that appeared in the shells, this being the method of their generation; and that, consequently, all the rest of this odd kind of fruit might be crabs in due time. To strengthen my conjecture, I have resolved to keep the weed in salt water, renewing it every day till we come onshore, by this exper iment to see whether any more crabs will be produced or not in this manner.

The next day, as he was changing the water, Ben found another crab much smaller than the one he had previously noticed, and this convinced him that his hypothesis about the weed was correct. But the weed could not live in a small pot of water; the rest of the embryos died. The following day Ben hauled in more gulfweed with a boathook, and found "three living, perfect crabs, each less than the nail of my little finger." He also noticed that one of them had "a thin piece of the white shell which I before noticed as their covering while they remained in the condition of embryos, sticking close to his natural shell upon his back."

Along with keen observation, Ben did some thinking about his own life. He was almost 21, and he decided it was time to reflect upon his experience and draw some conclusions from it. Thus far, he decided, his life had been like a bad play—"a confused variety of different scenes." He was now entering upon a new scene, and he decided to make some resolutions.

"1. It is necessary for me to be extremely frugal for some

time, till I have paid what I owe. [Thomas Denham had loaned him the money for the voyage home.]

"2. To endeavour to speak truth in every instance; to give nobody expectations that are not likely to be answered, but aim at sincerity in every word and action—the most amiable excellence in a rational being.

"3. To apply myself industriously to whatever business I take in hand, and not divert my mind from my business by any foolish project of growing suddenly rich; for industry and patience are the surest means of plenty.

"4. I resolve to speak ill of no man whatever, not even in a matter of truth; but rather by some means excuse the faults I hear charged upon others, and upon proper occasion speak all the good I know of everybody."

Arriving safely in Philadelphia, Ben discovered the "erratum" he had made with Miss Read had grown worse. In the confusion of his first months in London, he had written her only one letter, implying that it would be a long time before he came home. She had therefore contracted a marriage with another man, who turned out to be a drunkard. He soon fled Philadelphia for the West Indies, leaving behind him a small mountain of debts.

Seeing how unhappy he had made this young woman, Ben began thinking about why it had happened. He decided that his bad conduct had something to do with his skeptical attitude toward religion. He noted that his arguments against religion had convinced his friends Collins and Ralph, and each of them had "afterwards wrong'd me greatly without the least compunction." Governor Keith was another freethinker. In his skeptical days Ben had liked to argue that there was no such thing as morality. Now he began to think that certain actions might not be bad because God had forbidden them or good because He commanded them, but they might be forbidden because they were bad for us, or commanded because they were beneficial to us as human beings. Thus he became convinced, he told his son William, "that truth, sincerity and integrity in dealings between man and man were of the utmost importance."

Back in Philadelphia, Ben Franklin began practicing these principles. But he soon saw that bringing order and honesty into his personal life was only a first step. A single person, though sincere and industrious, could not accomplish very much. So Franklin formed a club, the Junto. He got the idea from a book by Cotton Mather, a famous Boston minister. The Junto met each Friday evening, and the rules that Franklin drew up required every member in turn to produce a set of queries on some important subject—such as politics, science or morality. These queries were discussed by the group, under the direction of a president. Once every three months, each member had to produce an essay on a subject that interested him. This too was discussed and debated by the group. Drawing on his own experience as a debater, Franklin had formulated rules which banned positive opinions and direct contradictions. Anyone who fell into either of these faults paid a small fine.

Along with the special queries that members were supposed to produce, there was a set of "standing queries," which members were asked to consider each week. Among them were the following:

"Hath any deserving stranger arrived in town since last meeting, that you heard of? And what have you heard or observed of his character or merits? And whether think you, it lies in the power of the Junto to oblige him, or to encourage him as he deserves.

"Do you know of any deserving young beginner lately set up, whom it lies in the power of the Junto any way to encourage?

"Have you lately observed any defect in the laws of your country? Or do you know of any beneficial law that is wanting?

"Have you lately observed any encroachment on the just liberties of the people?

These last two queries give us an interesting glimpse of what Ben Franklin was thinking around this time. Both of these ideas were to appear again and again in his life. Ben Franklin never stopped thinking about ways to improve the society in which he lived. And he never stopped worrying about the possibility that government, in the name of law and order, might take away the basic rights which every Englishman believed he had inherited at birth. Among these rights, or liberties, were trial by a jury of one's peers; the principle of habeas corpus, which forces a government to free a man from jail on the posting of reasonable bail; the right to petition the government for the redress of citizens' wrongs; and, above all, the right of free speech, which means that citizens can criticize the government in newspapers, in speeches and in conversations with their neighbors.

CHAPTER 4

THE NEWSPAPERMAN

MEANWHILE, BEN HAD TO COPE WITH SOME SUR-prising twists and turns in his career. Mr. Denham, the bene-factor who had brought him home from England, died six months after they returned to Philadelphia. Around the same time, Ben almost died too, from an attack of pleurisy. When he recovered, he decided to go back to the printing business again. He went to work as foreman for his old friend Keimer, but he soon saw that Keimer only planned to let him train his apprentices, and after they had learned printing, fire Ben, and so save the rather large salary he was paying him. Ben decided to go into business for himself.

He found a new friend, a Welshman named Hugh Meredith, who had a rather wealthy father. The older Meredith agreed to set them up in business as equal partners, if Ben would agree to train his son as a printer.

As soon as they opened their print shop, Ben began planning to publish a newspaper. There was only one paper in Philadelphia then, Andrew Bradford's *American Weekly Mercury*, a very inferior publication. But Keimer heard about Ben's plans, and rushed into print with another paper called *The Universal Instructor in All Arts and Sciences: and Pennsylvania Gazette*. Keimer could do nothing right—his paper was a disaster. It had little news in it; most of it was material reprinted from an encyclopedia. Franklin wrote a series of articles for the *Mercury*, ridiculing Keimer and his sheet, and soon the number of subscribers to the *Universal Instructor* . . . dwindled to the vanishing point. Within a year, Keimer announced he was leaving Pennsylvania, and sold the paper to Franklin and Meredith. Franklin promptly shortened Keimer's absurd title to *The Pennsylvania Gazette,* and went to work.

Already, Franklin had amazed easygoing Philadelphians with his energy. He regularly worked between twelve and fifteen hours a day. Meredith gave him little help. Printing bored him, and he preferred to sit around in nearby taverns drinking with friends. But because Meredith's father had put up the money to launch them, Franklin never criticized his lazy partner.

At first, Philadelphia's older merchants were sure that Franklin and Meredith would fail, because there were already two print shops in town. But one of the city's leading doctors, Patrick Baird, vigorously disagreed. "The industry of Franklin is superior to anything I ever saw of the kind," he said. "I see him still at work when I go home, and he is at work again before his neighbors are out of bed."

Finally, two friends went to Franklin separately, each unknown to the other, and offered him enough money to buy out his partner. Shrewdly, Franklin accepted half of each man's money, and easily persuaded Meredith to sell his share of the business. Meredith had realized he was not cut out to be a printer, and he and Ben parted in the friendliest fashion. Meredith took Franklin's money and bought a farm in North Carolina, where he lived happily for the rest of his life.

Franklin swiftly built the *Pennsylvania Gazette* into the best-known, most successful newspaper in America. One of the secrets of its popularity was the kind of wit which Franklin had already displayed in his Silence Dogood letters. The *Gazette* was always full of letters to the editor, some of which the editor wrote himself. There was Anthony Afterwit, who told sad stories about how his wife spent him into bankruptcy. Cecilia Single was a born shrew who lectured the editor in scorching terms because, she said, he was partial to men. Alice Addertongue said she was organizing a kind of stock exchange for the sale and transfer of calumnies and slanders.

Franklin carried on a long, lively war with his chief newspaper opposition, the *Mercury*. As usual, he scored points by making his readers laugh at his rival. He printed a letter from a man who declared himself the author of some verses published in the last edition of the *Mercury*. The fellow complained that for some unknown reason the editor of the *Mercury* had printed only the first two letters of his name, BL. "I request you to inform the publick that I did not desire my name should be concealed," declared the supposed author, "and that the remaining letters are O, C, K, H, E, A, D." Another letter pointed out that the *Mercury* had reported two prominent European soldiers had been killed by a single cannon ball—a remarkable achievement considering one of them was fighting in the Rhineland, and the other in Italy.

Equally important to the success of the *Pennsylvania Gazette* was Franklin's courage. In one of his first issues, he printed a story about the dispute which the assembly of Massachusetts was having with the royal governor, William Burnet. Franklin strongly supported the defiant stand of his native province, whose inhabitants insisted on their right to pay the Governor what they thought he needed and deserved. Boldly, the young editor applauded Massachusetts' refusal to knuckle under to the "menaces of a Governour fam'd for his cunning in politicks." Franklin said it was proof that Americans still retained "that ardent spirit of liberty, and that undaunted courage in the defense of it, which has in every age so gloriously distinguished BRITONS & ENGLISHMEN from all the rest of mankind." Later, Franklin proudly recalled how his bold stand had "struck the principal people" in Philadelphia and won him numerous new subscribers.

Inevitably, Franklin's independent attitude led him into conflict with the rulers of Pennsylvania. The province was a proprietary colony. Unlike a royal province, which was run by a governor appointed by the King, Pennsylvania was ruled by the sons of William Penn, the original proprietor, who had obtained the colony as a grant of land from the King, and then sold the lands within it to settlers, retaining millions of acres for his own property. As proprietors, Penn's two sons, Richard and Thomas, had the right to appoint the governor and his council, judges and other officials.

The proprietary party did not like criticism, and when Franklin began pointing out things that were wrong with the government, several friends advised him to follow a more cautious course. They warned that he and his paper would never be successful in Pennsylvania, without the power of the Penns behind him.

Franklin listened to this advice and invited these pessimists to dinner at his house that night. They sat down to a bare table, and the only food served to them was some strange looking mush in wooden bowls. Franklin poured some water into his bowl and began eating. His guests tried to follow his example, but the stuff tasted so terrible that they could barely swallow it. Finally, they asked him what in the world they were eating. "Sawdust meal and water," Franklin said. "Now go tell the rest of Philadelphia that a man who can eat that for supper doesn't need to be beholden to anyone."

Around this time, Franklin decided to marry. His choice was Deborah Read, the girl he had jilted when he went to London. He felt sorry for her and wanted to correct the "erratum" he had made in his relationship with her. He had also made another mistake since he returned to Philadelphia, which made it important for him to find an understanding wife. In spite of his resolution to lead a moral life, Franklin admitted in his *Autobiography* that he found it very difficult to control his sexual desires. Before he returned to Deborah, he had had a love affair with a very poor and rather ignorant woman. According to one story, she was an "oyster wench," selling oysters from a basket or a pushcart in the streets of the city. From this love affair, a son was born. Franklin named the boy William, and accepted complete responsibility for him. A child born out of wedlock is called illegitimate; people who speak more bluntly would call him a bastard. Franklin did not want his son to be raised with that label on him, and marriage to the boy's mother was out of the question. So, on September 1, 1730, Franklin married Deborah Read and brought his son into their household.

Deborah was grateful to Franklin for rescuing her from a lonely life and she did her best to accept William as her own son. She also worked hard for Franklin, who later recalled "how she assisted me cheerfully in my business, folding and stitching pamphlets, tending shop, purchasing old linen rags for the papermakers, etc., etc." He also proudly recalled that in those days he had been "clothed from head to foot in woolen and linen of my wife's manufacture." Deborah was also Franklin's financial bookkeeper and also ran the shop attached to his printing office, where he sold books and stationery.

Franklin was deeply grateful to Deborah, and showed it by writing a love song for her. One night, at the Junto, he and his friends had begun discussing how many love songs were written to mistresses, but no one had been able to think of a single song written in praise of a wife. The next day, Franklin gave this song to one of his friends, and asked him to memorize it and sing it at the next Junto meeting.

Of their Chloes and Phillises poets may prate
    I sing my plain country Joan
These twelve years my wife, still the joy of my life;
    Blest day that I made her my own.

Not a word of her face, or her shape, or her eyes
    Or of flames or of darts you shall hear;
Tho' I beauty admire 'tis virtue I prize
    That fades not in seventy year.

Some faults have we all, and so has my Joan
    But then they're exceedingly small;
And now I'm grown us'd to 'em, so like my own
    I scarcely can see 'em at all . . ."

CHAPTER 5

FIRST CITIZEN OF
PHILADELPHIA

TWO YEARS AFTER HIS MARRIAGE, WITH HIS paper thriving, Franklin launched an even more successful publication—*Poor Richard's Almanack*. Every newspaper publisher in the colonies tried to produce an almanac. It was an ideal way to use up "dead time" when the presses were standing idle, and if the book caught on it could also be profitable.

The success of an almanac depended upon the appeal of the "philomath"—the resident astrologer who did the writing and predicting. Franklin decided to become his own philomath. He realized that most people read an almanac for amusement and that they did not really believe that anyone could predict the weather and other events with any accuracy, a full year ahead. So Franklin created a philomath named

33

Richard Saunders, who wrote a funny introduction to the first almanac. Poor Richard explained that he only had taken to writing because his wife was sick of watching him gaze at the stars. She had ordered him to make some money, or she was going to burn all his books and instruments.

Franklin's competition in this field was an almanac written by a philomath named Titan Leeds. Solemnly, Poor Richard explained that he would have written almanacs long ago, but he hated to cut into his friend Titan's profits. Now, it was all right for him to publish, because Titan was about to die.

Richard explained that according to his reading of the stars, Titan would expire on October 17th, 1733, while Titan's calculations inclined him to think he would survive until the 26th of the same month. Naturally, Titan Leeds was infuriated, and wrote a nasty reply, insisting he was very much alive, and calling Poor Richard a fraud. The next year, Poor Richard replied. Titan Leeds was certainly dead, he declared, because in the almanac that appeared under his name for the year 1734 "I am treated in a very gross and unhandsome manner . . . I am called a false predictor, an ignorant, a conceited scribbler, a fool and a lyar." His good friend Titan would never have treated him this way. Titan continued to sputter insults, but his almanac soon faded in popularity, while Poor Richard's soared.

The main reason for Franklin's success were the proverbs which he strung throughout *Poor Richard's Almanack*. He took them from many books, including the Bible, but he often rewrote them to sharpen their wit or their point.

He's a fool that makes his doctor his heir.
Fish and visitors smell in three days.
The worst wheel of a cart makes the most noise.
Experience keeps a dear school, yet fools will learn at no
other.
It is hard for an empty sack to stand upright.
Sal laughs at everything you say; why? because she has
fine teeth.

Franklin also made fun of philomaths who pretended they could really predict the future. "I find that this will be a plentiful year of all manner of good things for those who have enough," he wrote, "but the orange trees in Greenland will go near to fare the worse for the cold. . . ."

Meanwhile, Franklin was working hard to improve Philadelphia. With the help of the Junto and the *Gazette,* he founded the city's first volunteer fire department and reorganized "The Watch," the city's policemen, who patrolled the streets at night. To give everyone a better chance to educate themselves, he founded a subscription library, the first in America. He was also the guiding spirit behind the creation of the Pennsylvania Hospital and the Philadelphia Academy, which eventually became the University of Pennsylvania. He helped to organize the colony's first militia, the Philadelphia Associaters, to provide a defense against a threatened French and Spanish invasion. At the same time, he served as clerk of the Pennsylvania Assembly.

In all of these areas, Franklin practiced a very unusual strategy of leadership. When he first began soliciting subscriptions for the library, he met with "objections and reluctances." He swiftly saw that others envied him, because they thought that he was tackling the job solely to get the credit for it. From that moment, Franklin put himself "as much as I could out of sight," and described the project as "a scheme of a number of friends" who had requested him to gather the support of "lovers of reading." The library was soon thriving, and henceforth, Franklin stayed behind the scenes, never attempting to take the credit or the glory for anything he achieved.

Only one thing marred Franklin's happiness. Two years after his marriage, Deborah had given birth to a son, whom Franklin named Francis Folger. At the age of four, the little boy died of smallpox. After this sad loss, Deborah became more and more jealous of William. She resented the attention Franklin showered on his only son. Franklin was a generous father. He bought William expensive presents, such as a pony, which the boy let wander away. Even after her daughter, Sarah, was born in 1743, Deborah still resented William's presence in the house. As he grew older, William could not help but notice that his stepmother did not like him, for Deborah had a very sharp tongue. Franklin did his best to soothe their quarrels, but he was not always successful.

At the same time, Franklin was thinking about his own

future. By 1745, he was a successful, moderately wealthy man, with an income of well over 2,000 pounds, or about $50,000, a year. (An ordinary working man considered himself lucky to make fifteen pounds a year.) He owned several houses in Philadelphia, and received rents from them. But Franklin saw no point in continuing to pile up more and more money. He called this "the pursuit of wealth to no purpose" and told a funny story about it. One day he visited a very wealthy Philadelphia friend, who took him through his expensive new house. The rooms were huge, and each time Franklin asked him why he had given himself so much space, the man replied, "Because I can afford it." Finally, Franklin smiled and said, "Why don't you buy a hat six times too big for your head? You can afford that too."

That kind of empty life was not for him, Franklin concluded. Instead, at the age of 42, he decided to retire from business. Not long before this he had hired a new printer, a Scotsman named David Hall. He was a very competent man and Franklin liked him, and he offered Hall a chance to become his partner, and run the business, if Hall would agree to pay Franklin half the profits from the *Pennsylvania Gazette* and *Poor Richard's Almanack* and other work done by the print shop for the next twenty years. At the end of that time, Hall would become the full owner of the business. Naturally, Hall leaped at the chance.

People in Philadelphia wondered what Franklin was going

to do. Some of his friends thought he was crazy to give up a profitable business that could have made him one of the richest men in America. They were even more amazed to discover that the retired Franklin was working harder than ever, but now he was not trying to make money. He was trying to solve the mysteries of electricity.

CHAPTER 6

SCIENTIST AND INVENTOR

TWO YEARS BEFORE, WHILE VISITING RELATIVES in Boston, Franklin had attended a lecture by Dr. Archibald Spencer, a Scottish scientist who had performed some electrical experiments. Later that year, Spencer had come to Philadelphia and sold most of his apparatus to Franklin. Franklin then bought more equipment through Peter Collinson, a Quaker friend in London who was a member of the Royal Society, the powerhouse of the British scientific world. Soon he was writing to Collinson, "I never was before engaged in any study that so totally engrossed my attention and my time as this has lately done."

At that time, scientists knew very little about electricity. They produced it by rubbing glass tubes with silk, or wool with resin. In 1746, at the University of Leyden, in the Netherlands, they discovered how to store electricity in a special bottle lined with strips of tin, that was soon called the Leyden jar. Most scientists thought there were two kinds of electricity, vitreous (from silk) and resinous (from resin). Franklin, experimenting in his Philadelphia laboratory, soon concluded that electricity was a single "fluid." But he noticed that sometimes it attracted, and sometimes it repelled. Why?

To answer that question, Franklin conducted the following experiment. He gathered three volunteers in his laboratory and had two of them, whom we shall call A and B, stand on wax squares, which insulated them from the ground. Then A rubbed a glass tube, thereby transferring some of the electricity in his own body to the tube. He then held the tube out to B, and immediately, an electric spark jumped from the tube to B's hand. Now A had less electricity than he normally possessed, and B had more than his usual share. Franklin now ordered B to hold out his hand to C, who was standing on the ground. Immediately, a spark leaped from B to C. Then Franklin repeated the experiment. However, this time he ordered B to ignore C, and to hold out his hand to A. A much greater electric spark jumped from B back to A.

The explanation? B's body, once he received the charge from A, had more electricity in it than he normally possessed. He was charged "positively," Franklin said. A, with less electricity, was charged "negatively." To simplify the explanation even more, Franklin called the positive charge plus and the negative charge minus. This was a major breakthrough in the history of electricity. It enabled scientists to understand for the first time how electrical current traveled from one body to another.

Franklin also noticed that a sharply pointed object, such as a knitting needle, drew off electricity from a positively charged body much more rapidly, and from a greater distance, than a blunt object.

Then, on November 7th, 1749, Franklin moved even closer to his greatest discovery. In a journal he was keeping of his experiments, he wrote, "Electrical fluid agrees with lightning in these particulars. 1. Giving light. 2. Colour of the light. 3. Crooked direction. 4. Swift motion. 5. Being conducted by metals. 6. Crack or noise in exploding. 7. Subsisting in water or ice. 8. Rending bodies it passes through. 9. Destroying animals. 10. Melting metals. 11. Firing inflammable substances. 12. Sulphureous smell. The electric fluid is attracted by points. We do not know whether this property is in lightning. But since they agree in all particulars wherein we can already compare them, is it not probable they agree likewise in this? Let the experiment be made."

Nine months later, he sent to Peter Collinson a letter summarizing his electrical discoveries and suggesting the experiment which he hoped would "make truth useful to mankind." He suggested erecting "on top of some high tower or steeple . . . a kind of sentry box." It would contain a man and an insulated stand. From the middle of the stand, an iron rod would rise and then, bending at right angles, pass out the door and go up again, twenty or thirty feet to a very sharp point. If clouds contained electricity, as Franklin suspected they did, the pointed rod would draw off the "fluid."

Franklin's letter was published in England as a small book entitled, *Experiments and Observations on Electricity, Made at Philadelphia in America*. It was translated into French, and soon two French electricians conducted Franklin's experiment, successfully drawing electricity from clouds. British electricians repeated the performance a few weeks later.

In America, meanwhile, Franklin tried another, more famous approach. Since there was no high ground or church steeple in or near Philadelphia, Franklin made a kite out of a silk kerchief, attached a pointed wire to the tip, and, accompanied only by his son William, went out to the Philadelphia commons, or public grazing grounds, on the edge of the town. There William got the kite aloft in a gathering thunderstorm. For insulation, Franklin tied the kite string to a silk ribbon which he held in his hand. Just above the ribbon he attached a key to the string.

At first, the kite dove and looped in the gathering storm, and nothing seemed to happen. But then, a scattering rain began to fall, and wet the string. Immediately, the fibers of the string stood erect, proof that they were positively charged. Franklin touched his knuckle to the key and received a mild electric shock. He then held the tip of a Leyden jar to the key, and drew off a large supply of electrical "fluid." He had been right. Clouds were full of electricity, and lightning and electricity were undoubtedly the same thing.

A few months later, in *Poor Richard's Almanack*, Franklin published the practical application of his idea. "It has pleased God in his goodness to mankind at length to discover to them the means of securing their habitations and other buildings from mischief by thunder and lightning." He then described how people could erect lightning rods on the roofs of their houses, and run them down the side of the building to the ground. The same thing could be done for ships, by running a wire from a rod on the mast down one of the shrouds to the water. The rod would thus "ground" to carry off the lightning charge harmlessly, instead of letting it hit the house or ship. Franklin made no attempt to patent his invention. He gave it to the world free of charge, as he did with many other things he invented, including the Pennsylvania fireplace, often called the Franklin stove. This was the first fireplace that kept most of the warm air in the room, instead of letting it escape up the chimney. Franklin also invented the first electrical battery. And he redesigned the street lights of Philadelphia, substituting four flat panes of glass for a globe, which quickly became smoky and gave little light. All of these things he gave to the world, free of charge, remarking that he had profited in his life from the inventions of other men, and that was why he had no desire to make money from his own inventions.

Franklin's electrical discoveries, particularly his work with lightning and the lightning rod, made him world famous. The King of France sent his personal congratulations across the ocean. The British Royal Society elected him a member by unanimous vote and bestowed upon him its highest award, the Copley Medal. Yale and Harvard gave him honorary degrees. Immanuel Kant, the greatest philosopher of the time, compared him to Prometheus, the Greek god who had brought down fire from heaven and gave it to mankind. In 1750, most people still believed that there was something divine about lightning, associating it with the vengeance of an angry God. The man who tamed it readily acquired an awesome, almost superhuman image.

But Franklin declined to act like a superman. Instead, he delighted in entertaining his friends with electrical tricks. He would electrify a many-legged piece of wire, and make it walk like a spider. He darkened the room, and electrified the gold border of a book. He electrified the gold crown on a painting of England's king, George II. Anyone who touched it received a very strong shock. He put a glass of brandy on one side of the Schuylkill River and sent an electric current across the river to set it ablaze. He electrified the gold rims of glasses, and then let his friends drink wine from them, giving them a tingling shock. He killed turkeys with a shock from his electric battery, and roasted them on an electric jack. Once, to show electricity's power, he knocked down three strong men with a single charge.

During one of these exhibitions, Franklin almost killed himself. He was showing a group of visitors how he could kill a turkey. Conversing with them while he prepared his apparatus, he accidentally touched the positive and negative poles at the same time. There was a loud crack, and Franklin's body vibrated like that of a man having a convulsion. He blacked out completely for several seconds, but, amazingly, did not fall. The hand that received the electric charge was dead white, and there was a bruise on his breastbone as if he had been hit there by a rock. Otherwise, he was unharmed, and he made a joke out of the incident. "I was going to kill a turkey," he said, "but it seems that I almost killed a goose."

Stories about Franklin's experiments attracted curiosity-seekers by the dozens. They would lurk around his house, trying to catch a glimpse of the electrician in his laboratory. One day Franklin electrified the rail fence on which they leaned, and sent a hefty charge surging down it. The gawkers vanished in a cloud of dust, certain that the devil himself had gotten inside them.

Franklin spent four years studying electricity, and at the end of that time he had transformed it from a curiosity into a branch of science. If he had been able to continue his study of it, he might have achieved even more scientific triumphs.

But there were political problems in Pennsylvania which badly needed solving, and Franklin could not resist his friends when they asked for his help. He believed that solving political and moral problems was more important than making scientific discoveries. He was fond of saying that if Isaac Newton, one of England's greatest scientists, had been the captain of a ship, he would not have been justified if he deserted the helm in a crisis to make even the greatest of his scientific discoveries.

The welfare of a colony such as Pennsylvania, which had over 300,000 people in it, was an even heavier responsibility. Franklin felt that every citizen in a free society shared the responsibility for its safety and health. Franklin also felt deeply grateful to Pennsylvania for giving him a chance to rise from poverty and obscurity to modest wealth and fame, and he wanted to give others the same opportunity. So, when his fellow citizens elected him to the Assembly as a representative from Philadelphia, Ben Franklin more or less abandoned his laboratory and put his powerful mind and considerable energy to work on the politics of Pennsylvania.

The Penns were the big problem in Pennsylvania. They owned millions of acres of land in the colony, but they refused to pay any taxes on them. Each time a governor was sent from England, he had specific instructions to veto any bill passed by the Assembly taxing the proprietors' estates.

Particularly annoying was the Penns' refusal to share the expenses of dealing with the Indians. Each year Pennsylvania and the other colonies gave the tribes on their respective frontiers expensive presents to keep them loyal and at peace. The French, in possession of Canada, began competing for the Indians' support with even more expensive presents. This was an unfortunate development for the colonies because the French, united in a single colony with the immense wealth of the French king behind them, were easily able to outbid individual colonies, such as Pennsylvania. One of Franklin's first duties as an assemblyman was to serve as a commissioner to negotiate new treaties of peace with Pennsylvania's Indians. When he and his fellow commissioners found out that the Indians considered their offerings inadequate, they promptly advanced their own money to buy more goods "at the Philadelphia price" on the frontier.

Franklin returned from this conference deeply worried about the future of England's colonies in America. He thought their very existence was imperiled by France's aggressive plans to move down the Ohio and seal off the colonies between the Appalachian Mountains and the Atlantic Ocean. It was time for the English colonies to unite. He pointed out to his friends that the Iroquois, a confederation of six Indian tribes, was the strongest power in the Indian world. Why didn't the English follow their example?

"It would be a strange thing if six nations of ignorant savages should be capable of forming a scheme for such an union, and be able to execute it in such a manner as that it has subsisted ages and appears indissoluble; and yet that a like union should be impracticable for ten or a dozen English colonies, to whom it is more necessary and must be more advantageous. . . ."

More and more, Franklin began thinking of the thirteen English colonies as a nation that must be formed.

CHAPTER 7

THE POSTMASTER

EVEN BEFORE HE BEGAN STUDYING ELECTRICITY, Franklin had tried to unite Americans who had a common interest in science by founding the American Philosophical Society. Its purpose was to pool scientific knowledge and to speed up its application to American life. The response was disappointing, partly because of the wretched mail service in the colonies. It took as long as six weeks for a letter to travel from Boston to Philadelphia, and letters were frequently lost by careless post riders and postmasters. It was hard to unite people who had trouble communicating with each other, and Franklin soon began thinking of ways to improve the postal service.

First he took the job of postmaster in Philadelphia, partly to make sure that his newspaper, which had the largest circulation of any on the continent, was regularly and safely mailed to subscribers. Then in 1751, the Deputy Postmaster General for America died, and Franklin applied for his job. He got the appointment, and swiftly went to work to transform the American postal system. For four years he worked at it without making a cent of money. Only if the system showed a profit would he get paid, and for decades it had been operating at a loss.

Like the scientist that he was, Franklin preferred to learn from first-hand observation, and within a few months after his appointment, he set out on a ten-week journey "to the East," as he called it, in the language of the born Bostonian. He traveled across New Jersey, through New York, and up into Connecticut, Rhode Island, and Massachusetts.

The improvements Franklin achieved in the postal service were nothing less than spectacular. He reduced the traveling time of a Boston-Philadelphia letter from six weeks to three. Abolishing the old monopolistic system by which each postmaster sent the newspaper of his choice through the mail free, he opened the service to all papers, for a small charge. He insisted on postmasters keeping precise accounts of their revenues and ordered them to print in the newspapers the names of persons who had letters waiting for them—a practice he had long followed in Philadelphia. People who did not call for their letters on the day they arrived had them delivered the following day, and were charged an extra penny. Again, this was an innovation Franklin had tried first in Philadelphia, and it made the post office much more popular. Too often in many cities, letters were allowed to lie around for weeks, and were liable to be lost, or read by idlers. After three months, unclaimed letters were forwarded to the central post office in Philadelphia—thus creating the first dead-letter office.

On the post roads, Franklin had milestones erected, so that post riders could pace themselves better. By talking with riders and postmasters face to face, Franklin established an esprit de corps, which had much to do with getting a new vitality into the service. He consulted the post riders and post-masters on new roads, fords, and ferries. In three years, the service was completely overhauled, and its new speed and reliability won it a popularity it had never known before. In the fourth year of Franklin's administration, it paid a profit for the first time in its history, collecting more revenue in 12 months than it had in the previous 36.

Traveling was a rugged business in the 1750s, and only someone with Franklin's tough constitution could have endured the bad weather, the terrible roads (too often either quagmires of mud or suffocating dust storms), the innumer-able rivers which the traveler had to ford or ferry. Taverns and inns were few and often overcrowded. To get a place by the fire, after hours on the road in rain or cold, was difficult.

Once Franklin used his wit to overcome this particular challenge. Stopping in a Rhode Island tavern on a raw, blustery, rainy day, he found two dozen locals and travelers crowded around the room's only fire.

"Boy," Franklin said in stentorian tones to the tavern-keeper's son, "get my horse a quart of oysters."

"A quart of oysters?" gasped the boy.

"You heard me, a quart of oysters," Franklin boomed.

The boy obeyed, and there was a general stampede out the door to see this incredible phenomenon, a horse who ate oysters. The horse snorted and snuffled in indignation, and refused to have anything to do with the oysters. Baffled, the curiosity-seekers trooped back into the tavern, to find Deputy Postmaster General Franklin sitting serenely in the chair closest to the fire.

While Franklin traveled around America, his mind was not idle. In fact, moving from colony to colony inspired him to set down on paper one of his most important scientific insights, published a few years later under the title, "Observations Concerning the Increase of Mankind, Peopling of Countries &c." With a brilliant combination of mathematics and social observation, Franklin noted that there were now well over 1,000,000 Englishmen in North America. Yet little more than 80,000 had emigrated from England. This fact alone showed a radical difference between the New World and the Old World, where population was relatively stable. America, with its almost unlimited land and productive capacity, placed no barrier to marriage and the raising of families, as the economically cramped Old World did. For this reason, Franklin predicted that the population of America would double every 20 or 25 years—a prophecy which was fulfilled with scientific exactitude until 1860, when massive immigration created even more rapid growth. For Franklin, contemplating this increase in the early 1750s, it meant one significant thing— America will "in another century be more than the people of England, and the greatest number of Englishmen will be on this side of the water."

Franklin did not see this as a threat to the mother country. He boldly spoke and wrote as an Anglo-American and loyal member of the Empire. "What an accession of power to the British Empire by sea as well as land! What increase of trade and navigation! What numbers of ships and seamen!" Underlying this emotion, however, was a more uniquely American sentiment. In 1750, Parliament had restricted the manufacture of iron in Pennsylvania, because British ironmasters had complained that American-made iron was competing with their products. This made no sense to Franklin, because the population of the colonies was increasing so fast that there was sure to be an ever-growing market for manufacturers, whether British or American. "A wise and good mother," Franklin said, placed no distressing restraints on her children. "To distress is to weaken, and weakening the children weakens the whole family."

Franklin was not afraid to speak boldly when he confronted British stupidity. Shortly after he finished his essay on population, he sarcastically suggested a way for Americans to stop another bad British practice. Whenever their jails became overcrowded, the British deported their criminals to America.

Often these evildoers continued their life of crime in the New World, committing numerous robberies and murders. The best way to solve the problem, Franklin suggested in the *Pennsylvania Gazette,* was to return the compliment. From now on, let the Americans regularly export all their rattlesnakes to England.

Because as Deputy Postmaster General he was one of the few Americans who thought in terms of the entire continent, Franklin was appointed by Pennsylvania to be a delegate to the Albany Congress, convened in 1754 to work out a common intercolonial defense against the threatening French and Indians. Typically, he did more than think defensively. He proposed a plan of union which would have created a Governor General and a Grand Council consisting of members chosen by the assemblies of each colony. Although the delegates to the conference approved the plan, it received short shrift both from the colonial assemblies and from England. The colonial assemblies thought that it conceded too much of their local power to the General Council and especially to the Governor General, who would be appointed by the King. London thought it came too close to creating a political body strong enough to challenge the power of Parliament.

Disappointed, Franklin nevertheless continued to try to drum up interest in the idea wherever he went. He found an ardent listener in William Shirley, the royal governor of Massachusetts. The two men had many conversations together and also exchanged several letters on the subject.

Shirley's approach, natural enough for a man who saw the colonies through the eyes of the Crown, was to have the Grand Council work out plans for common defense and pay for them from taxes laid on the Americans by an act of Parliament. Worse, Shirley's Grand Council consisted largely of Royal Governors and their councilors, all of whom were appointed by the King, or at least required his approval.

Franklin immediately warned Shirley that Americans would never tolerate this approach. "Excluding the people of the colonies from all share in the choice of the Grand Council would probably give extreme dissatisfaction, as well as the taxing them by act of Parliament where they have no representation." In three searching letters, which were really political essays, Franklin explained to the Governor why Americans would not pay taxes voted by Parliament, and why they resented England's interference in their internal affairs. More than two decades later, James Madison, reading these letters, declared that Franklin had summed up the entire argument of the American Revolution "within the compass of a nutshell" 20 years before it occurred to anyone else.

CHAPTER 8

FATHER

PENNSYLVANIA, AND HIS FAMILY, REMAINED AT least as important to Franklin during these years as his post-mastering and continental politicking. When Franklin took his seat in the Pennsylvania Assembly, he resigned his job as Assembly clerk, which he had held for over a dozen years. The Assembly promptly appointed William Franklin as his replacement. It was one more evidence of the central place William held in Franklin's affections. If a single word had to be chosen to describe Benjamin Franklin, paternal would come close to saying it all. This burly, broad-shouldered man seemed to fulfill himself most when he was in fathering role, sharing his strength, his wisdom, his generosity, and his humor with other people. Inevitably, this brought a special intensity to his relationship with his only son.

Another reason for this intensity was William's uneasy

position in Philadelphia society. As Franklin's political power increased, he became more and more critical of the petty grasping policy of the Penns. This made him an antagonist of the members of the proprietary party, who held the judgeships and other positions of power and honor which the Penns could bestow. Unable to wound Franklin personally, they struck at him through his son. There were constant snide whispers about William's illegitimate birth. When he fell in love with pretty, poetically talented Elizabeth Graeme, and asked for her hand in marriage, her wealthy parents haughtily rebuffed him. Inevitably, it saddened Franklin to see his son forced to cope with such unpleasant experiences.

Another reason why Franklin worried over William was the young man's relationship with Deborah, who continued to unleash her shrew's temper on her stepson.

A young clerk named Daniel Fisher, who lived in Franklin's house for a time, has left us a vivid picture of Deborah Franklin's feelings toward William. In his diary, Fisher wrote of seeing young Franklin pass through the house "without the least compliment between Mrs. Franklin and him or any sort of notice taken of each other." One day, as Deborah was chatting with Fisher, and William Franklin passed them in silence as usual, Deborah Franklin exclaimed, "Mr. Fisher, there goes the greatest villain upon earth." While Fisher stared in bewilderment, Deborah proceeded to denounce William Franklin "in the foulest terms I ever heard from a gentlewoman." Young Fisher eventually quit his job and moved out of the Franklin household. He simply could not stand Deborah Franklin's "turbulent temper."

Deborah and her husband had slowly moved apart, in the years since their marriage. She remained the shopkeeper's daughter, practically illiterate. She would sign her letters to him, "Your affecthone wife." He always began his letters to her: "My dear child." More and more jealous of the time he gave to public affairs, she told Daniel Fisher, "All the world claimed a privilege of troubling her Pappy," her family name for Franklin.

Eventually, Franklin gave up trying to control Deborah's wild tongue. With his father's permission, as soon as William obtained his first salary as clerk of the Assembly the young man moved into separate quarters to escape his quarrelsome stepmother.

In his teens, William had toyed with escaping Philadelphia and Deborah for good. He had tried to run away as a sailor aboard a privateer. Returned home through Franklin's intervention, he had badgered his father into getting him an army commission and had marched off to fight the French in Canada. The war ended before he heard a shot fired in anger, but he came home with a military style in his bearing, and an aura of adventure which gave him more self-confidence in his relationships with young Philadelphians his own age.

Almost immediately, William embarked on another, far more significant adventure. With fur trader George Croghan, he traveled west to an Indian conference on the Ohio. Like many other Americans of his generation, young Franklin was struck by the fabulous richness of the land beyond the Alleghenies, and the almost boundless abundance of it. He poured out his story about "the country back of us" to his father, who listened with keen interest, and was so impressed he sent copies of William's journal to friends in England.

William was convinced that a fortune was waiting for the men who first possessed these lands, then so haphazardly "owned" by small bands of Indians, who regarded them only as hunting preserves. In fact, when he returned home, he talked of nothing but ways of organizing trading companies and colonizing expeditions which would establish England's grip on the territory. For a while, Ohio seemed to be the only thing that interested him, aside from the pursuit of Philadelphia's belles at the Assembly Balls.

Finally, Franklin took William aside, and bluntly informed him that Ohio, fascinating and important as it might some day become, was at the moment about as substantial as a castle in the clouds. What Franklin feared was the possibility that William was assuming he could invest his time in fantasies and Assembly Balls because he was eventually coming into a handsome inheritance. Gently, Franklin told his son that he planned to spend the modest estate he had accumulated on himself. William had better start thinking about choosing a profession.

Shortly after the great kite experiment, William began studying law in the office of Franklin's good friend and political lieutenant, stocky, learned Joseph Galloway. At the same time, Franklin wrote to England and asked friends there to register William in the Inns of Court, where the elite of the British legal profession studied the common law. Hopefully, he said, he would make the trip to England with William when the time came for him to go.

CHAPTER 9

FRONTIERSMAN

BEFORE THEY WENT TO ENGLAND, HOWEVER, Franklin and his son shared a wild adventure on the Pennsylvania frontier. The French had built a fort on the site of the present-day city of Pittsburgh. To drive them out, the British sent Major General James Braddock and an army of 2,500 red-coated regulars. Pennsylvania and the other colonies were supposed to contribute money to purchase supplies for this army, but instead, the Pennsylvanians got into their usual wrangle with the Governor about taxing the Penns' estates. This made Braddock very angry with Pennsylvania, and the Assembly sent Franklin and his son William to Frederick, Maryland, where Braddock was organizing his troops and gathering his supplies, to explain the situation.

The Franklins arrived to discover General Braddock almost

insane with fury. The supplies sold to the army by American contractors were rotten, and there were only 25 wagons collected to transport tents and supplies for 2,250 men. Braddock was damning everyone involved, from the ministers in England who thought up the expedition to the haggling farmers who would not risk a wagon in the service of their country. The two Franklins watched while earnest young George Washington of Virginia, who was serving as General Braddock's aide, argued in vain with the General, trying to defend America's reputation.

Hoping to calm the general down, Franklin assured him that there were plenty of wagons available in Pennsylvania. The desperate general seized him by the arm. "Then you, sir, who are a man of interest there can probably procure them for us, and I beg you will undertake it." The General took a hundred pounds in hard cash from his money box and told Franklin to get to work.

The two Franklins immediately conferred with Sir John Sinclair, Braddock's quartermaster general. He had just returned from Pennsylvania, and he was angrily criticizing everything about the colony. Franklin noticed that Sinclair had a special uniform, which resembled that of a Hussar, the fearsome light cavalry of the Austrian and German armies, famous for their love of plunder.

Quickly Franklin dashed off a handbill, and had several thousand copies printed for distribution throughout Lancaster, York and Cumberland counties. He offered 15 shillings a day (perhaps $100 in modern money values)—a good price for a wagon, four horses and a driver. But the heart of Franklin's message was his warning that if the farmers of Pennsylvania did not accept "such good pay and reasonable terms" their loyalty would be "strongly suspected." This would put the King's "brave troops" in an exceedingly bad mood, and their march through the counties would almost certainly be "attended with many and great inconveniences."

If General Braddock did not get the necessary number of wagons in fourteen days, "I suppose Sir John Sinclair, the Hussar, with a body of soldiers, will immediately enter the province . . . which I shall be sorry to hear, because I am very sincerely and truthfully your friend and well-wisher."

Since most of the farmers in these counties were German immigrants, the word "Hussar" had an almost magical effect on them. Well within the deadline, over 150 four-horsed wagons, plus 259 pack horses, streamed into Braddock's camp.

The two Franklins became General Braddock's favorite dinner guests. He discussed his battle strategy with them, and Benjamin Franklin did not like what he heard. He warned the General that his army, struggling through the thick forests and over the swift streams of western Pennsylvania, would be easy to ambush. General Braddock laughed at this remark. "The savages may indeed be a formidable enemy to your raw American militia," said the British commander in chief, "but upon the King's regular and disciplin'd troops, sir, it is impossible that they should make any impression."

Benjamin and William Franklin rode home to Philadelphia, their minds still troubled by doubts. A few days later, two doctors, old friends of Franklin, came to him asking him to donate money to buy several hundred pounds of fireworks to celebrate the capture of Fort Duquesne, Braddock's objective in western Pennsylvania. Franklin let his glasses slip down a little on his nose and said, "I think it will be time enough to prepare the rejoicing when we know we have a reason to rejoice."

The doctors looked amazed. Like General Braddock, they assumed that British regulars were invincible. "Why the devil," said one of them, "you surely don't suppose that the fort will not be taken."

"I don't know that it will not be taken," Franklin said, "but I know that war is a very uncertain business."

The doctors abandoned their fund-raising. A few days later, a messenger rushed into Philadelphia carrying the stunning news that Braddock had been ambushed only a few miles from Fort Duquesne and two-thirds of his army killed or wounded. The survivors, under the command of Colonel Thomas Dunbar, were in headlong retreat.

The British did not stop running until they got to Trenton, New Jersey, on the eastern side of the Delaware. Obviously, it was up to Pennsylvania to defend its frontiers as best it could All Braddock had accomplished was to build a handsome road down which the French and Indians could now pour, unrestrained, to slaughter hapless farmers and their families in their lonely cabins.

But not even desperate necessity could reconcile the Penns and Pennsylvania's Assembly. Again and again, the family's appointed representative, Governor Robert Hunter Morris, vetoed every tax bill which included the Proprietors' estates. Throughout the summer and the fall, debate raged, while the Indians on the frontier picked off isolated farms and single travelers in small, probing raids. When not even a sign of resistance appeared, the savages grew bolder. Large raiding parties poured into Berks and Northampton counties, and people died under the hatchet and scalping knife less than eighty miles from Philadelphia.

Most of the victims were Germans. Frantically they begged Governor Morris for help and when they got no answer, more than a thousand of them marched on Philadelphia, carrying a wagon full of scalped corpses which they parked before the Governor's mansion. Fortunately, the Penns had only a few days earlier offered to donate 5,000 pounds to the defense of the colony, if the Assembly would agree to a money bill that did not tax their estates. Under Franklin's leadership, the Assembly voted 60,000 pounds to raise and equip troops. But volunteers came forward very slowly. The bill exempted Quakers from serving—it was against their religion to serve in the army—and most other Pennsylvanians were reluctant to risk their lives to defend these apostles of nonviolence.

Franklin attacked the problem in the *Pennsylvania Gazette*, in the form of a dialogue among citizens X, Y, and Z.

"For my part," said Z, "I am no coward; but hang me if I'll fight to save the Quakers."

X replied, "That is to say you won't pump ship because it'll save the rats as well as yourself."

Then late in November came the worst news yet from the still defenseless frontier. The German village of Gnadenhutten had been surprised by a Shawnee war party and every living soul slaughtered except a handful who escaped to the woods. The victims had all been pacifists, like the Quakers. Pure terror swept Pennsylvania. Farmers and their families abandoned their homesteads and crowded into the villages. Governor Morris was forced to beg Franklin to raise and organize a force of 300 rangers and lead them to the frontier.

Franklin accepted. He knew little about military affairs, but he knew how to lead men. With William Franklin taking care of the military details, Franklin marched his Rangers to the frontier, organized militia in a number of panic-stricken towns, and then advanced to Gnadenhutten, slogging through bitter cold and sleety rain. He spent his 50th birthday in a German farmer's barn, soaking wet from an all-day march in the rain. Indians sniped at them from a distance, but the braves had no stomach for taking on Franklin's well-armed force.

The Indians watched from the hills while Franklin and his son directed the little army in the building of a sturdy fort.

Franklin noticed that on the days that the men worked hard they were "good-natured and cheerful," while on days when rain forced them to be idle, they were mutinous and quarrelsome, "finding fault with their pork, the bread, etc., and in continual ill-humour."

The small army had a chaplain, a Presbyterian named Charles Beatty, who came to Franklin complaining that the men "did not generally attend his prayers and exhortations." As a stern soldier of the Lord, he was probably hoping that Franklin would issue an order, forcing the men to worship under threat of punishment. Instead, Franklin suggested that the chaplain double as steward of the rum. (The men were guaranteed a gill of rum a day, half in the morning and half in the evening.) He advised Chaplain Beatty to deal out the rum after prayers, and the chaplain took his advice. "Never were prayers more generally and more punctually attended," said Franklin.

The frontier secured, the Franklins returned to Philadelphia. There they found only more bitterness between the Assembly and the Proprietary Party. The 5,000 pounds which the Penns had supposedly donated to the war effort consisted of back rents in Pennsylvania which the Assembly would have to collect. Franklin led the Assembly in a mass march through the streets to deliver a scorching "remonstrance" to the Governor. When that official insisted on following his instructions, the Assembly ripped off another resolution, "That a commissioner or commissioners be appointed to go home to England, in behalf of the people of this province, to solicit a removal of the grievances we labor under by reason of Proprietary instructions." Benjamin Franklin was chosen to tackle this job. He asked William to go with him, to serve as his chief assistant—and also to complete his law studies at the Inns of Court, in London.

CHAPTER 10

SPOKESMAN FOR
PHILADELPHIA

THE FRANKLINS RENTED ROOMS IN A HOUSE ON Craven Street, just off The Strand, one of the most fashionable streets in London, and only a few blocks away from the government offices in Whitehall Palace and the Houses of Parliament. The house was owned by a charming widow, Margaret Stevenson, who had a pretty young daughter, Polly. Franklin soon converted the Stevensons into a second family; Polly became a daughter to him. She was a brilliant girl, and Franklin encouraged her to study science, and to ask him questions about it. During the next several years he wrote her numerous letters about scientific topics, such as why black cloth absorbs more heat than white cloth. But as usual, he did not believe anyone should study science to the point where they did not lead a normal life. He urged Polly to marry and raise a family, soon making it clear, in fact, that he had strong hopes that William would propose to her, and that she would become his daughter-in-law.

But William was too busy enjoying London's high life. He did not particularly like an independent, studious girl like Polly. He preferred a more clinging, dependent woman and he soon found one in Elizabeth Downes, the daughter of a West Indian planter. She was pretty, and had a sweet, gentle disposition. But she declined to marry William as long as he had no visible means of support. William had to depend on Benjamin Franklin for all his considerable expenses. At one point, perhaps a little shocked by adding up how much he had spent recently, William told his father, "I am extremely oblig'd to you for your care in supplying me with money," and assured his father he would never forget his "paternal affection."

William continued his studies in the law at the Inns of Courts. Like his father before him, he found it hard to control his sexual drives, and soon he was forced to inform Franklin that he was a grandfather. A son, whom William named William Temple, had been born to a woman whom historians have never identified. Franklin insisted that his son accept complete responsibility for the boy, and advanced him the money needed to place the child with a good family in the country, who would raise him until it was time for him to go to school.

Meanwhile, with William's help, Franklin easily routed the

Penns, and forced them to agree to let their lands be taxed by the Pennsylvania Assembly. To this triumph, Franklin added a personal one. Through numerous friends around the British throne, he won for William an appointment as the Royal Governor of New Jersey.

William's appointment was part of a master plan that Franklin was evolving, to run the Penns out of Pennsylvania and replace them with a royal governor directly under the rule of the Crown. What better argument for royal government, than to be able to point to the honest, stable, peaceful regime of that staunch son of Philadelphia, William Franklin, Governor of New Jersey?

Finally, there was another, even larger dream. Franklin had never forgotten William's vivid description of the Ohio Valley. With the French defeated, this now was English territory. Already he had discussed with powerful friends in England the possibility of founding a colony there as William Penn had founded Pennsylvania. What better way to train his son in the uses of power, than to inherit the immense responsibility which this political experiment would leave him?

Perhaps the best example of Franklin's amazing ability to win friends in England was the letter which William Strahan, the richest and most powerful printer in London, publisher of an influential newspaper and of books such as Samuel Johnson's famed dictionary, wrote to Franklin's partner David Hall. In Franklin's six years in England, his friendship had become the most important relationship in Strahan's life, outside of his family.

Strahan began by telling "Dear Davie" (Hall had worked as an apprentice for him before joining Franklin in Philadelphia) that Hall would never have seen Franklin's face on his side of the water "had my power been in any measure equal to my inclination." It was amazing, Strahan went on, the way Franklin with all his remarkable talents and abilities which had won the admiration and affection of "the greatest geniuses of this country" was equally beloved by simple businessmen such as himself. Franklin knew how "to level himself for the time to the understandings of his company, and to enter without affectation into their amusements and chitchat." This was how he made people from all walks and levels of life "his affectionate friends."

As for himself, Strahan said, "I never found a person in my whole life more thoroughly to my mind . . . It would much exceed the bounds of a letter to tell you in how many views, and on how many accounts, I esteem and love him . . . Suffice it to say that I part with him with infinite regret and sorrow. I know not where to find his equal, nor can the chasm his departure leaves in my social enjoyments and happiness ever be filled up. There is something in his leaving us even more cruel than a separation by death; it is like an *untimely death,* where we part with a friend to meet no more, with a *whole heart,* as we say in Scotland." Strahan went on for pages, lamenting "a separation so much the more bitter and agonizing, as it is likely to be endless."

Franklin's affection for Strahan was deep enough. He told him, in his farewell letter, that he felt so depressed on leaving England, he had to admit that Strahan's "persuasions and arguments" had had their effect. "The attraction of reason is at present for the other side of the water, but that of inclination will be for this side. You know which usually prevails. I shall probably make but this one vibration and settle here forever. Nothing will prevent it, if I can, as I hope I can, prevail with Mrs. F. to accompany me."

Back in America, Franklin supervised the installation of William as Royal Governor of New Jersey, and did his utmost to persuade Deborah to return to England with him. He had fallen so totally in love with the mother country, he was serious about spending the rest of his life there. In a letter to an English friend he exclaimed, "Why should that petty island, which compared to America is but like a stepping stone in a brook, scarce enough of it above water to keep one's shoes dry; why, I say, should that little island, enjoy in almost every neighborhood, more sensible, virtuous and elegant minds, than we can collect in ranging a hundred leagues of our vast forests?" From Philadelphia he assured Strahan, "In two years at farthest I hope to settle all my affairs in such a manner, as that I may then conveniently remove to England, provided we can persuade the good woman to cross the seas."

But the good woman absolutely refused to consider an

ocean crossing. Deborah had an hysterical fear of ships and water, similar to the phobia that prevents many people from flying today. So, regretfully, Franklin began building a handsome new house in Philadelphia, and Governor William Franklin was soon telling the disconsolate Strahan that his father was obviously planning to spend his old age in America.

By now Franklin was 59, definitely old in a century when most men died in their 40s and 50s, with only a handful reaching the biblical three score and ten. Yet Franklin did not look or act old. He still had the burly, bulky vigor of his middle age, in spite of a paunch which sometimes prompted him to call himself "Dr. Fatsides."

When an Indian war erupted on the Pennsylvania frontier, the need to tax the Penns' estates again became a ticklish problem in the colony's Assembly. Franklin, who had been elected in absentia during his years in England, prepared the taxation bill in strict accordance with the agreement he had reached with the Penns. Then, to his disgust he discovered that the Penns had instructed their governor not to permit any taxation on their lands that exceeded the lowest taxes paid by individual owners on the poorest, cheapest land in the colony.

Infuriated but calm, Franklin marshaled his forces, and rammed through a bill petitioning the King to take the government of Pennsylvania out of the venal hands of the Penns, once and for all. Over the desperate opposition of the proprietary party, the Assembly appointed Franklin their delegate to take the petition to London and win its approval from the King and his Privy Councilors. Franklin assured the agitated Deborah that he would be back within twelve months. Then, escorted by no less than 300 men on horseback, he rode down to Chester on the Delaware, where the ship, *King of Prussia,* was waiting for him. Cannon, borrowed from the Philadelphia armory, boomed as he went aboard and the crowd sang an improvised version of "God Save the King."

> O LORD our GOD arise,
> Scatter our Enemies,
>   And make them fall.
> Confound their Politicks,
> Frustrate such Hypocrites,
> Franklin, on Thee we fix,
>   GOD Save us all
> Thy Knowledge rich in Store,
> On Pennsylvania pour,
>   Thou *(sic)* great Blessing
> Long to defend our Laws,
> Still give us greater Cause,
> To sing with Heart and Voice,
>   GEORGE and FRANKLIN
> GOD Save Great GEORGE our King;
> Prosper agent FRANKLIN:
>   Grant him Success:
> Hark how the Vallies ring;
> GOD Save our Gracious King,

From whom all Blessings spring,
Our Wrongs redress.

Franklin's devoted political lieutenant, Joseph Galloway, and two other close friends, Thomas Wharton and Abel James, both prominent Philadelphia merchants, went on board ship with him and sailed down the Delaware to New Castle. Franklin was deeply touched by this outpouring of affection and loyalty. On the night of November 8th, alone in his cabin aboard the *King of Prussia,* he had only one worry which still nagged at his mind: his daughter, Sarah, whom he called Sally. At 21, she was almost certain to be exposed to the same kind of humiliating snubs and petty insults from her father's political enemies that had made William Franklin unhappy. Benjamin had wanted to take Sally with him to England, to put her beyond the reach of this revenge, at least for the year he expected to be gone. But Deborah Franklin had absolutely refused to part with her.

Before the ship sailed, Franklin wrote Sally a letter, assuring her of his love and giving her some wise advice. He urged her to ignore the nasty things his enemies were saying about him. Even the pastor of the church that Sally attended was anti-Franklin, and made cruel remarks about him from the pulpit. Nevertheless, Franklin urged Sally to continue to attend church. Otherwise, his enemies would use her absence to accuse her of being a bad woman, like her evil father. Finally, he urged her to acquire "those useful accomplishments, arithmetick and bookkeeping." With the Philadelphia establishment so thoroughly aroused against the Franklins, there was not much chance that Sally would marry a wealthy scion. So Franklin was attempting to prepare her for becoming a tradesman's wife, and wanted her to be able to give her husband the kind of valuable help Deborah had given him.

Franklin had no need to worry about William, of course. He was happily married to the Englishwoman he had met in London, and making a great success of his governorship in New Jersey. Franklin was tremendously proud of him.

When the elder Franklin sailed, he had every reason to believe that his mission would be successful. With the many friends he had acquired in England, he was confident he could drive the Penns out of Pennsylvania, and get the government's approval of a new colony in the Ohio Valley. Together, he and his son would build a model society there. Benjamin Franklin had no way of knowing that instead he was sailing into a maelstrom that would destroy his relationship with William—the deepest and most important personal relationship in his life.

CHAPTER 11

PERSUADER OF PARLIAMENT

WHEN FRANKLIN REACHED ENGLAND EARLY IN December, 1764, he found himself involved in a completely unexpected political uproar. The British government was deeply in debt, for it had cost over 200 million pounds to defeat France in the Seven Years War. British politicians shuddered at the thought of trying to impose more taxes in England, Scotland or Ireland. Everyone there was already complaining that the taxes were too high.

It was also costing the British a lot of money to maintain an army in America to control the Indians, and they decided to make the Americans pay for this expense, by taxing them. When Franklin arrived, he found Parliament preparing to pass a Stamp Act for America. All legal documents, marriage licenses, wills, contracts, as well as newspapers and many other items, would henceforth be required to carry a Royal stamp, which the government would sell. A similar law was already in existence in England.

Franklin and three other Americans went to see George Grenville, England's First Minister (the leader of the British cabinet, now called the Prime Minister), to advise him against passing the law. They warned him that Americans would resent it. They did not believe that Parliament had a right to tax them, because they had no representatives in Parliament. But Grenville did not listen to them. He presented the bill to Parliament, and it was passed with practically no debate. Franklin advised his American friends to be patient. He and other Americans in England would begin work to get the law repealed, but it might take a long time.

The reaction in America was much more impatient. In almost every colony, assemblies condemned the bill. In Virginia, Patrick Henry, a young backwoods orator, arose in the House of Burgesses to thunder, "Caesar had his Brutus, Charles I his Cromwell, let George III profit from their example." In Boston and New York, mobs rioted, destroying the houses of government officials, and forcing commissioners appointed by the Crown to sell the stamps, to resign. In Philadelphia, Franklin's proprietary party enemies spread a vicious rumor that he was in favor of the Stamp Act, and had even helped the British government draft the law. A mob gathered in the streets, and threatened to attack his house.

Franklin, in London, heard the story from Deborah, in vivid, if badly spelled letters. For nine days, she said, she was kept in "one contineued hurrey" by people urging her to flee with her daughter Sally to Governor William Franklin's home in Burlington, New Jersey. But other friends and relatives staunchly supported them. One of Deborah's cousins arrived to tell her that "more than twenty pepel" had told him it was his duty to stay with her. She told him she was "pleased to receive civility from aney bodey."

Toward nightfall, Deborah told her cousin to "fech a gun or two" and also to summon her brother to assist in the defense of the house. "We maid one room into a magazin. I ordored sum sorte of defens up stairs such as I cold manaig my selef," Deborah told her husband. When neighbors again advised her to flee, she refused. "I sed . . . I was verey shuer you had dun nothing to hurte aney bodey nor had I not given aney ofense to aney person att all nor wold I be maid unesey by aney bodey nor wold I stir or show the leste uneseynis." Reinforcements from other relatives and Franklin's friends and neighbors, all well armed, discouraged the mob, and Franklin's house was not attacked.

In London, Franklin redoubled his efforts to get the Stamp Act repealed. He had letters from friends in America published in the newspapers, warning the English that they were in danger of losing the colonies. Franklin himself spent long hours at his desk, answering the arrogant and opinionated assaults on Americans that began appearing in the English press. He also worked tirelessly to influence members of Parliament. Almost every hour of the day, Franklin told one friend, was spent in "forming, explaining, consulting, disputing" with Britain's lawmakers. He worked closely with a committee of 28 London merchants who pressured Parliament to repeal the Stamp Act. Americans had signed non-importation agreements, pledging themselves to buy no English goods until the tax was repealed. The merchants sent circular letters to 20 other British towns and cities urging them to petition Parliament to abandon the Stamp Act before it wrecked the British economy.

At first, Franklin seemed to make little progress. Many members of Parliament saw the Stamp Act as a test of Parliament's right to tax Americans. "A peppercorn, in acknowledgement of the right, was of more value than millions without," one said.

Edmund Burke, a brilliant Irish-born member of Parliament who wanted to repeal the Stamp Act, decided Parliament needed to be better informed. "Ignorance of American affairs," he declared, had misled them. So he summoned a series of experts before Parliament to testify about America. One of these was Benjamin Franklin.

Franklin made sure that his testimony would have a real impact. With the help of several friends in Parliament, he drew up and carefully rehearsed a list of questions and answers that he hoped would refute the Stamp Act once and for all.

On February 13, 1766, Franklin appeared before the House of Commons. His testimony demolished the supporters of the

Stamp Act. Refuting the notion that America was rich, and relatively untaxed, Franklin told how many taxes Americans were already paying to their colonial assemblies. Even more effective was the way he showed that the Stamp Act was not only unjust, but totally impractical. In the thinly populated back settlements along the frontier, and in Canada (now an English possession), there was no mail service, and people could not get stamps—which meant they could not marry, make their wills, or buy or sell property without taking long journeys and "spending perhaps three or four pounds, that the Crown might get sixpence."

At one point, Franklin won a bitter exchange with George Grenville himself, the man who had proposed the Stamp Act. Out of office now, Grenville was angry at anyone who dared to criticize his brainchild. "Do you think it right that America should be protected by this country and pay no part of the expense?" he demanded.

"That is not the case," Franklin replied. "The colonies raised, clothed, and paid during the last war, near 25,000 men, and spent many millions."

"Were you not reimbursed by Parliament?"

"We were only reimbursed what in your opinion we had advanced beyond our proportion, or beyond what might reasonably be expected from us; and it was a very small part of what we spent. Pennsylvania, in particular, disbursed about 500,000 pounds and the reimbursements in the whole did not exceed 60,000 pounds."

Grenville sat down, looking very uncomfortable.

In answer to the prepared questions from his friends, Franklin presented some significant statistics about the population of America, and how much the colonists imported from Britain. There were 300,000 men in America between 16 and 60—more than enough to make a formidable army. Pennsylvania alone imported 500,000 pounds of British goods each year. The implication was obvious. Not only would a war with these people be dangerous; it would be highly uneconomic.

On and on the questions and answers rolled, drawing from Franklin answers that made the Stamp Act look more and more like the greatest piece of idiocy in Parliament's history. The supporters of the Stamp Act become so enraged, they began asking stupid questions.

Would the colonies acquiesce in the authority of Parliament if the Stamp Act was repealed? One man huffed.

"I don't doubt at all that if the legislature repealed the Act the colonies will acquiesce in the authority," said Franklin with a twinkle in his eye.

But Franklin closed his performance with a solemn warning.

"If the Act is not repealed, what do you think will be the consequences?" asked one of his friends.

"A total loss of the respect and affection the people of America bear this country, and of all the commerce that depends on that respect and affection."

A week later, the House of Commons voted to repeal the

Stamp Act. In America, the news touched off a wave of celebrations. Franklin's testimony before Parliament was reprinted in almost every colony, and his popularity soared. The proprietary party in Pennsylvania had to eat the slander they had been spreading, that Franklin had aided and abetted the Stamp Act.

But in London, the man who made the victory possible was not so optimistic about the future. He noted wryly that Parliament had also passed a Declaratory Act, in which it insisted that it had the right to enact laws binding the British colonies "in all cases whatsoever." Only a few weeks later, Parliament renewed the law that gave England the power to export convicts to the colonies. Franklin quietly circulated among his friends another bill, which would have given the colonies the right to export their convicts to Scotland. Most of the members of Parliament who saw it laughed, and considered it a joke. Obviously, they did not get Franklin's basic message, which was serious. The Americans were not going to let the British push them around indefinitely.

CHAPTER 12

AGENT

AFTER THE STAMP ACT UPROAR, THERE WAS NO hope of driving the Penns out of Pennsylvania and substituting a Royal Governor. But Franklin stayed on in London, as Pennsylvania's agent. The people felt that no one could do a better job of representing them before the various boards and committees that ran the empire.

Also, he was working on a plan to create a paper currency for all the colonies in America. Not only would it help to unify them, but it would also increase the circulation of money, and thus stimulate business. In Franklin's plan, the British government would derive a small profit from selling the money to the colonies, which would be a painless and invisible form of taxation. But as usual, he found it hard to get anyone in the British government to take his advice. America was only one part of the great British Empire. There were also the colonies in India, Africa, and the West Indies which claimed much of the government's attention. And the English political scene was very turbulent, with new cabinets and new First Ministers coming in and out almost every year.

At the same time, Franklin worked to create one of his oldest dreams, a new colony in the Ohio River Valley. William Franklin was now even more deeply involved in this dream. In America, Governor Franklin had joined some friends his own age in a company that negotiated a treaty with the Indians, giving them access to some of this land. In London, Franklin tried to win the British government's approval. Eventually, he persuaded William and his friends to dissolve their American company and merge it with a larger British company, which Franklin and his friends formed in London. Franklin drew into this company some of the biggest names in the British establishment. Lord Gower, the president of the King's Privy Council, was a partner. Slowly, patiently, for five years Franklin worked on this project.

Almost every year, he would tell his wife or his son William that he was discouraged and eager to return home. But something always happened to keep him in England for another year. If it was not the hope of some progress on the Ohio colony, it was new turmoil between England and America.

In 1768, Charles Townshend, one of the more lightheaded members of Parliament, proposed a series of new taxes. Instead of the internal tax of the Stamp Act, the Townshend Acts placed heavy duties on paper, lead, glass and other commodities that the colonies imported from England. Americans resented these taxes, and immediately began agitating for their repeal. Again, Franklin was busy writing articles in British newspapers, defending America against bitter accusations from angry Britons.

More and more, he became a spokesman for all Americans, and not just for Pennsylvania. Georgia asked him to be their agent in London, and then New Jersey, no doubt prompted by Governor William Franklin, made the same request. Then came a real surprise. Massachusetts, the most rebellious of all the colonies, asked Franklin to represent them.

Actually, it was the Massachusetts Assembly that made this request. The Assembly had been feuding furiously with the Royal Governor, Thomas Hutchinson, over the Townshend Acts and other matters. When the London agent for Massachusetts died, the choice of a new agent became part of the wrangle. It soon became obvious that the Governor and the Assembly could not agree on a new man, so the Assembly chose Franklin as its representative, and told the Governor to get his own agent.

Franklin knew that serving as agent for Massachusetts was a very dangerous job. Since they were the most independent of all the colonies, anyone who represented them was bound to be disliked by the men in power in London. Accepting the job was doubly painful for him, because he knew it might ruin his chances of getting approval for the Ohio colony. But he accepted the appointment, because he believed that the people of Massachusetts and their fellow Americans in other colonies were right, and the British were wrong, in the debate over Parliament's power.

Franklin found out just how much trouble Massachusetts was likely to cause for him when he went to see Wills Hill, Lord Hillsborough, the Minister in charge of the American colonies. Franklin had already tangled with him over the Ohio colony, which Lord Hillsborough did not approve. He had huge estates in Northern Ireland, and he was afraid that a new colony in America might lure workers away from that country. But Franklin had pushed the project steadily, in spite of Lord Hillsborough's disapproval, and had made considerable progress when he went to call on his lordship, on January 16th, 1771, to present his credentials as the agent for the Massachusetts Assembly. Here is a blow-by-blow account of the stormy interview, written by Benjamin Franklin only a few hours after it took place.

I was shown into the levee room, where . . . several other gentlemen were there attending, with whom I sat down a few minutes, when Secretary Pownall came out to us, and said his Lordship desired I would come in.

I was pleased with this ready admission and preference, having sometimes waited three or four hours for my turn; and, being pleased, I could more easily put on the open, cheerful countenance, that my friends advised me to wear. His Lordship came towards me and said, "I was dressing in order to go to court; but, hearing that you were at the door, who are a man of business, I determined to see you immediately." I thanked his Lordship, and said that my business at present was not much; it was only to pay my respects to his Lordship, and to acquaint him with my appointment by the House of Representatives of Massachusetts Bay to be their agent here, in which station if I could be of any service—(I was going to say—"to the public, I should be very happy"; but his Lordship, whose countenance changed at my naming that province, cut me short by saying, with something between a smile and a sneer,)

L.H. I must set you right there, Mr. Franklin, you are not agent.

B F. Why, my Lord?

L.H. You are not appointed.

B.F. I do not understand your Lordship; I have the appointment in my pocket.

L.H. You are mistaken; I have later and better advices. I have a letter from Governor Hutchinson; he would not give his assent to the bill.

B.F. There was no bill, my Lord; it was a vote of the House.

L.H. There was a bill presented to the governor for the purpose of appointing you and another, one Dr. Lee, I think he is called, to which the governor refused his assent.

B.F. I cannot understand this, my Lord; I think there must be some mistake in it. Is your Lordship quite sure that you have such a letter?

L.H. I will convince you of it directly. *(Rings the bell.)* Mr. Pownall will come in and satisfy you.

B.F. It is not necessary, that I should now detain your Lordship from dressing. You are going to court. I will wait on your Lordship another time.

L.H. No, stay; he will come immediately. *(To the servant.)* Tell Mr. Pownall I want him.

(Mr. Pownall comes in.)

L.H. Have not you at hand Governor Hutchinson's letter, mentioning his refusing his assent to the bill for appointing Dr. Franklin agent?

Sec. P. My Lord?

L.H. Is there not such a letter?

Sec. P. No, my Lord; there is a letter relating to some bill for the payment of a salary to Mr. De Berdt, and I think to some other agent, to which the governor had refused his assent.

L.H. And is there nothing in the letter to the purpose I mention?

Sec. P. No, my Lord.

B.F. I thought it could not well be, my Lord; as my letters are by the last ships, and they mention no such thing. Here is the authentic copy of the vote of the House appointing me, in which there is no mention of any act intended. Will your Lordship please to look at it? *(With seeming unwillingness he takes it, but does not look into it.)*

L.H. Any information of this kind is not properly brought to me as Secretary of State. The Board of Trade is the proper place.

B.F. I will leave the paper then with Mr. Pownall to be—

L.H. *(Hastily.)* To what end would you leave it with him?

B.F. To be entered on the minutes of that Board, as usual.

L.H. *(Angrily.)* It shall not be entered there. No such paper shall be entered there, while I have any thing to do with the business of that Board. The House of Representatives has no right to appoint an agent. We shall take no notice of any agents, but such as are appointed by acts of Assembly, to which the governor gives his assent. We have confusion enough already. Here is one agent appointed by the Council, another by the House of Representatives. Which of these is agent for the province? An agent appointed by act of Assembly we can understand. No other will be attended to for the future, I can assure you.

B.F. I cannot conceive, my Lord, why the consent of the governor should be thought necessary to the appointment of an agent for the people. It seems to me that—

L.H. *(With a mixed look of anger and contempt.)* I shall not enter into a dispute with YOU, Sir, upon this subject.

B.F. I beg your Lordship's pardon; I do not presume to dispute with your Lordship; I would only say, that it seems to me, that every body of men, who cannot appear in person, where business relating to them may be transacted, should have a right to appear by an agent. The concurrence of the governor does not seem to me necessary. It is the business of the people, that is to be done; he is not one of them; he is himself an agent.

L.H. *(Hastily.)* Whose agent is he?

B.F. The King's, my Lord.

L.H. No such matter. He is one of the corporation by the province charter. No agent can be appointed but by an act, nor any act pass without his assent. Besides, this proceeding is directly contrary to express instructions.

B.F. I did not know there had been such instructions. I am not concerned in any offence against them, and—

L.H. Yes, your offering such a paper to be entered is an offence against them. *(Folding it up again without having read a word of it.)* No such appointment shall be entered. When I came into the administration of American affairs, I found them in great disorder. By *my firmness* they are now something mended; and, while I have the honor to hold the seals, I shall continue the same conduct, the same *firmness.* I think my duty to the master I serve, and to the government of this nation, requires it of me. If that conduct is not approved, *they* may take my office from me when they please. I shall make them a bow, and thank them; I shall resign with pleasure. That gentleman knows it, *(pointing to Mr. Pownall,)* but, while I continue in it, I shall resolutely persevere in the same FIRMNESS. *(Spoken with great warmth, and turning pale in his discourse, as if he was angry at something or somebody besides the agent, and of more consequence to himself.)*

    B.F. *(Reaching out his hand for the paper, which his Lordship returned to him.)* I beg your Lordship's pardon for taking up so much of your time. It is, I believe, of no great importance whether the appointment is acknowledged or not, for I have not the least conception that an agent can *at present* be of any use to any of the colonies. I shall therefore give your Lordship no further trouble. *(Withdrew.)*

Franklin soon evened the score with Lord Hillsborough, however. He forced him to hold a hearing on the Ohio colony. The Board of Trade, which Hillsborough also headed, issued a report disapproving the project. Franklin requested the Privy Council to review this decision, and they repudiated Hillsborough's report. Completely humiliated, Hillsborough resigned. But he remained a powerful enemy, and his friends in the government stalled the final decision on the colony.

On April 6th, 1773, Franklin wrote an amusing letter to his friend and partner, Joseph Galloway, about this slow progress. "The affair of the [Ohio] grant goes on but slowly. I do not yet clearly see land. I begin to be a little of the sailor's mind when they were handing a cable out of a store into a ship, and one of 'em said: ' 'Tis a long heavy cable. I wish we could see the end of it.'

" 'D——n me,' says another, 'if I believe it has any end; somebody has cut it off.' "

CHAPTER 13

THE JOKER

WHILE HE WAS FIGHTING ON ALL THESE FRONTS, Franklin also managed to enjoy himself, and to remain keenly interested in his family and friends, keeping in close touch with his wife and daughter, in America. Only after a good deal of hesitation did he agree to Sally's marriage to Richard Bache, an emigrant from Yorkshire, in England. Bache returned to England to introduce himself to his father-in-law, and Franklin loaned him money to help him get started as a merchant in Philadelphia. Later came news that delighted him: Sally had made him a grandfather, and named the boy Benjamin Franklin Bache.

Franklin immediately warned his wife not to spoil the new arrival. He told her a story of two little boys in the street. "One was crying bitterly; the other came to him to ask what was the matter? I have been, says he, for a penny worth of vinegar, and

I have broke the glass and spilt the vinegar, and my mother will whip me. No, she won't whip you, says the other. Have then you got ne'er a grandmother?"

At Craven Street, where he stayed with the Stevensons, Franklin was equally pleased when Polly married a gifted young doctor, William Hewson. When she had a child, she promptly made Franklin the godfather. She wrote Franklin regularly, telling him of the child's progress. Franklin, in turn, gave her amusing advice on how to raise him. "Pray let him have everything he likes; I think it of great consequence while the features of the countenance are forming; it gives them a pleasant air, and, that being once become natural and fix'd by habit, the face is ever after the handsomer for it, and on that much of a person's good fortune and success in life may depend. Had I been cross'd as much in my infant likings and inclinations as you know I have been of late years, I should have been, I was going to say, not near so handsome; but as the vanity of that expression would offend other folks' vanity, I change it, out of regard to them, and say a great deal more homely."

Franklin was always teasing Polly and her friends to give him a kiss or a hug. His favorite among these friends was Dolly Blount, a very pretty young woman. Next door to Franklin lived James Hutton, one of the leaders of the Moravian Church in England, who also enjoyed pursuing Miss Blount for a kiss. One day, another of Polly's friends informed Franklin and Hutton that Dolly had made a vow to marry whichever one of them became a widower first. "It is impossible to express the various agitations of mind appearing in both their faces on this occasion," Franklin wrote, laughing at himself as much as at Hutton. "Vanity at the preference given them over the rest of mankind; affection to their present wives, fear of losing them, hope, if they must lose them, to obtain the proposed comforts; jealousy of each other in case both wives should die together, &c, &c,—all working at the same time jumbled their features into inexplicable confusion. They parted at length with professions & outward appearances indeed of ever-during friendship, but it was shrewdly suspected that each of them sincerely wished health & long life to the other's wife; & that however long either of these friends might like to live himself, the other would be very well pleas'd to survive him."

When he was not enjoying himself at Craven Street, Franklin often visited the homes of wealthy and powerful Englishmen. Among these, his two favorites were William Petty, Lord Shelburne, and Francis Dashwood, Lord le Despencer, the head of the British post office. Shelburne was sympathetic to America's side in the argument with Parliament, and he had favored the Ohio colony, until a shift in the political power structure had driven him out of office. He was now a member of the opposition, as the British called the party out of power in Parliament.

One weekend at Bowood, Shelburne's estate (which still stands, not far from London), Franklin played a joke on the assemblage of famous guests, including members of Parliament and the noted actor David Garrick. Walking in the "park," the broad landscaped gardens of the estate, Franklin remarked that he had acquired unusual powers, thanks to some scientific experiments he had been making. For instance, he now could transform rough water into calm water, at a wave of his cane. Of course, no one believed him. They pointed to a nearby brook, where a breeze was stirring up many small waves, and told him to prove it. Franklin walked over to the side of the brook and passed his cane over it a few times. The spectators gasped with disbelief—the surface of the water suddenly became calm, and as glassy as a mirror.

A workman, who was standing nearby, was sure that Franklin had just demonstrated supernatural powers. "What should I believe?" he cried.

"Only what you see," Franklin said.

The rest of the spectators rushed to the bank, and begged Franklin to tell them how he had done it. Only then did he reveal that the botton of his cane was hollow, and in the hollow he carried a small vial of clear oil. Franklin had been experimenting with the use of oil to calm storms at sea, in the hope of aiding vessels in distress. He found that it did not work very well on the ocean, but it did an excellent job on smaller bodies of water.

Another weekend at Lord le Despencer's, Franklin enjoyed the pleasure of seeing one of his best political jokes throw everyone into a turmoil. In one of the London papers under the heading of foreign news, he published, "An Edict from the King of Prussia." The Edict, supposedly signed by Frederick the Great of Prussia, declared that henceforth Prussia was going to exercise more control over its colony, England. The right to call England a colony was based, the King said, on the fact that it had been settled hundreds of years ago by German tribesmen. The King proceeded to forbid the manufacture of iron and numerous other products in exactly the same way that the English Parliament forbade their manufacture in America. All goods shipped by England had to pass through the German port of Koningsberg, just as all American ships had to touch first at London, and pay a duty on their cargoes before going on to other countries. Finally, the Edict declared, "We do hereby also ordain and command, that all the *thieves*, highway and street robbers, housebreakers, forgers, murderers . . . and villains of every denomination, who have forfeited their lives to the law in Prussia; but whom we, in our great clemency, do not think fit here to hang, shall be emptied out of our gaols into the said island of Great Britain, for the better peopling of that country."

Franklin was sitting in the breakfast room at Lord le Despencer's estate, when a visiting writer, Paul Whitehead, rushed into the room with the newspaper containing the Edict in his hand. "Here," he said, "here's news for ye! Here's the King of Prussia, claiming a right to this kingdom."

All stared with astonishment, and Franklin managed to look as surprised as the rest of the company.

Whitehead proceeded to read two or three paragraphs. "Damn his impudence," roared another guest, "I dare say, we shall hear by next post that he is upon his march with 100,000 men to back this." But then Whitehead, noticing the frequent references to Britain and the American colonies in the Prussian king's justification of his Edict, suddenly squinted at Franklin and said, "I'll be hanged if this is not some of your American jokes upon us."

Franklin cheerfully admitted his guilt, and Whitehead proceeded to read the rest of the Edict to roars of laughter. Everyone agreed that it was "a fair hit." Lord le Despencer liked the piece so much he had it cut out of the paper and preserved in his library.

In the summer or the fall of each year, Franklin took a trip, for he found that it improved his health to escape from London's sooty atmosphere for five or six weeks. But even on these trips, he found it more and more difficult to avoid politics. This was especially true in the fall of 1771, when he made a tour of Ireland and Scotland. He was appalled by the poverty he saw, especially in Ireland which was completely dominated by the English. To a friend in Rhode Island, he wrote vividly of what he had seen and why it convinced him that America must maintain its rights in the face of Parliament's grasping power.

"I have lately made a tour thro Ireland and Scotland. In those countries, a small part of the society are landlords, great noblemen, and gentlemen, extreamly opulent, living in the highest affluence and magnificence: the bulk of the people tenants, extreamly poor, living in the most sordid wretched-ness, in dirty hovels of mud and straw, and cloathed only in rags.

"I often thought of the happiness of New England, where every man is a freeholder, has a vote in public affairs, lives in a tidy, warm house, has plenty of good food and fewel, with whole cloathes from head to foot, the manufacture perhaps of his own family. Long may they continue in this situation!"

Because he was determined to keep America free, Franklin decided to do something very risky. During one of his visits with English friends, a powerful member of the British government began arguing with him about the feud between Massachusetts and the Crown. To Franklin's amazement, the man assured him that the harsh policies which the British government had adopted—stationing troops there, forcing the Assembly to meet at inconvenient places, making judges inde-pendent of the people by having the Crown pay their salaries—had all been suggested by Americans, men living in Massachusetts. Franklin demanded proof, and his British friend produced for him letters which Governor Thomas Hutchinson and his Lieutenant Governor Andrew Oliver had written to a British official, recommending these and even harsher measures. "There must be some abridgment of what is called English liberty" in the colonies, Hutchinson had written.

Franklin, satisfied that the letters were authentic, decided to send them to his friends in Massachusetts. He felt it was his duty as agent to do so, in spite of the fact that the letters had obviously been stolen from the house of the man to whom they had been written, shortly after his death. Franklin said he hoped to make Americans realize that the quarrel between England and America was not all England's fault.

Franklin's strategy might have worked, if there had been time for Americans to think about what the Hutchinson-Oliver letters meant. But other things happened, almost at the same time, which combined with the letters to help start the Revolution.

CHAPTER 14

THE REVOLUTIONARY

DISTURBED BY AMERICAN RESISTANCE TO THE Townshend Acts, Parliament had repealed all of them except the tax on tea. This was retained to "uphold the right"—the right of Parliament to tax the colonies. The tax was very small, only threepence to a pound, but Americans refused to pay it as a matter of principle. Sales of British tea, imported from India by the East India Company, plummeted. Americans preferred to drink illegal tea, smuggled from the French and Dutch West Indies.

The East India Company lost millions of pounds, as tea piled up in its warehouses in England. Its stock tumbled on the London Exchange, and many people who had bought it went bankrupt.

Watching the spectacle, Franklin blamed the whole thing on British pride and greed. More and more, as he watched the

British government's behavior toward America, he became convinced that the English were scheming to reduce Americans to the kind of brutal poverty they had inflicted on Ireland. They wanted to create a vast network of government jobs which they could parcel out to their friends as they regularly did jobs in the Irish government.

Franklin stated this opinion boldly in the British newspapers, and in letters to friends in America. By this time the government was interrupting his mail regularly. The British soon began to regard Franklin as the man behind the entire American resistance. To some extent this was true. His letters were reprinted regularly in newspapers up and down the continent. As Deputy Postmaster General, he could send letters free by writing "Free B. Franklin" on them. But now, to make sure Americans got his message, he began writing "B. free Franklin."

Meanwhile, the Thomas Hutchinson letters which Franklin had sent to Massachusetts created political explosion in that colony. Franklin had asked his friends to show them only to a handful of influential leaders. But some of these men circulated them far beyond this small group, and soon they were printed in the newspapers. The Massachusetts Assembly passed a resolution demanding Hutchinson's removal as governor and sent it to Benjamin Franklin for presentation to the King. Franklin submitted it, and the Privy Council scheduled a hearing on the matter.

While Franklin was out of town, two men, one an American,

the other the brother of the man to whom the letters were written, fought a duel over them. The brother, whose name was Thomas Whately, accused the American, John Temple, of stealing them. The duel ended with Whately slightly wounded and demanding another match. Franklin, anxious to avoid bloodshed, published a letter in London's leading newspaper, admitting he had procured the letters and sent them to America. This admission aroused all his enemies in the British government.

Then came even more inflammatory news from America. The British government, trying to help the East India Company, had given them permission to sell their tea at a price so low that Americans would find it hard to resist. The tax remained on the tea, however. This angered many Americans who were determined to deny Parliament's right to tax the colonies. So, when the tea ships arrived carrying their cargoes of specially priced tea, riots took place in numerous ports. Unfortunately for Franklin, the first news of these acts of defiance to reach England came from Boston. There, a group of rioters, disguised as Indians, had boarded the tea ships, broken open the chests of tea, and thrown the contents into the harbor.

The leaders of the British government, already angry with Franklin, were now totally furious. At the Privy Council hearing on the petition to remove Hutchinson, they arranged for his public humiliation. The government Solicitor General, a lean, sharp-tongued Scot named Alexander Wedderburn, was "hired" as Hutchinson's defense attorney. While the full Privy Council of 35 lords, as well as their numerous followers, lady friends, and courtiers, snickered and guffawed, Wedderburn called Franklin a thief, a liar, an intriguing revolutionary—just about every dirty name in the English language.

Franklin stood a few feet away, absolutely silent, his face expressionless, throughout this hail of abuse. One American who happened to be present, a hot-blooded South Carolinian, marveled at Franklin's self-control. "Had it been me that was so grossly insulted, I should instantly have repelled the attack, in defiance of every consequence," he said. Later, Franklin told his friends that he had never before appreciated the value of a good conscience. If he had not been absolutely convinced that what he had done with the Hutchinson letters was right, he could never have endured the ordeal.

The next day, Franklin was informed by letter that he was dismissed as Deputy Postmaster General for North America. His first thoughts were of the fatal consequences to the Ohio Colony, and to his son's career. He immediately resigned from the Ohio Colony board so that no one could use him as an excuse to deny the final approval of the grant of land.

In a letter to William Franklin written just after his humiliation before the Privy Council, Franklin advised: "As there is no prospect of your being ever promoted to a better government, and that you hold has never defrayed its expenses, I wish you were well settled in your farm. 'Tis an honester and a more honourable, because a more independent employment."

Two weeks later, however, he wrote to his son in a calmer frame of mind. "Some tell me that it is determined to displace you likewise, but I do not know it as certain . . . Perhaps they may expect that your resentment of their treatment of me may induce you to resign, and save them the shame of depriving you when they ought to promote. But this I would not advise you to do. Let them take your place if they want it, though in truth I think it is scarce worth your keeping . . . But one may make something of an injury, nothing of a resignation."

Already Franklin was convinced that a revolution was inevitable and that America would become an independent nation. He wanted his son William to play a large part in the government of this new nation. William could indeed "make something" of an injury from the British government.

But it soon became apparent that the British were planning to injure a lot of other Americans before they got around to William Franklin. To punish Boston for the Tea Party, the Ministry proposed and Parliament swiftly passed a series of bills which the Americans called the Intolerable Acts. One closed the port of Boston to all shipping, until the tea was paid for. Another provided that any Royal official accused of murder or a similar crime would be tried outside Massachusetts, or in England. A third bill virtually annulled the colony's charter, giving the Governor almost dictatorial powers, and making him answerable for his salary, and the exercise of his power, only to England.

Finally came a blow that was to some extent aimed directly at Franklin. The Quebec Act set up a government for the French in Canada, and extended the borders of Canada southward to the Ohio River, swallowing Franklin's proposed colony. The Americans immediately saw that the British were attempting to pin them between the mountains and the sea. Alexander Wedderburn admitted as much, when members of the opposition accused the government of this intention, in debates in Parliament over the bills to punish Boston. For Franklin these Intolerable Acts were additional proof that the British were planning to reduce America to the state of total oppression with which they reigned in Ireland.

In America, the Intolerable Acts had a dramatic and almost immediate effect on public opinion. Everyone realized that if the British could change one colony's charter, they could change every colony's charter. From Connecticut to Georgia, Americans rallied to Massachusetts' side in the argument. Food and money poured into Boston to sustain the thousands of people who were jobless, because of the closing of the port. At the same time, the leaders of the colonies decided to convene a Continental Congress in Philadelphia to discuss the crisis and to work out ways to maintain a united front against the British.

In London, the British government was stunned by this surge of American support for Massachusetts. Franklin kept his American friends informed. "The coolness, temper & firmness of the American proceedings; the unanimity of all the colonies . . . have a good deal surprized and disappointed our enemies," he wrote.

Franklin was more worried by ominous signs of trouble in his relationship with his son. Governor Franklin, as a Royal official, did not look on the Continental Congress favorably. Instead, he suggested a congress of Royal Governors to mediate the quarrel. He also urged his father to come home to tell Americans that they should make peace with England.

Franklin could barely conceal his annoyance. "You say my presence is wish'd for at the Congress," he wrote, "but no person besides in America has given me the least intimation of such a desire; and it is thought by the great friends of the colonies here, that I ought to stay till the result of the Congress arrives, when my presence here may be of use." Curtly, he told William, "I hear nothing of the proposal you have made for a congress of Governors, &c." Franklin also did not like a remark that William had made, that the citizens of Massachusetts ought to think of "doing justice before they ask it" and pay for the ruined tea. Franklin vehemently disagreed. "They have extorted many thousand pounds from America unconstitutionally, under colour of acts of Parliament, and with an armed force. Of this money they ought to make restitution. They might first have taken out payment for the tea, &c., and returned the rest. But you, who are a thorough courtier, see everything with government eyes. . . ."

Again and again, Franklin exhorted his countrymen to

maintain their resistance. "By its continuance, you will undoubtedly carry all your points: by giving way you will lose every thing. Strong chains will be forged for you, and you will be made to pay for both the iron and the workmanship . . . If you should ever tamely submit to the yoke prepared for you, you cannot conceive how much you will be despised here, even by those who are endeavouring to impose it on you."

Not everyone in the British government wanted war with America. When they saw that Americans were almost unanimously determined to resist Parliament's claim, several members of the government, including the First Minister Lord North, approached Franklin secretly, through private messengers. Two Quaker friends, David Barclay and Dr. John Fothergill, asked him if he would draw up a plan to settle the quarrel, stating the principal American demands in ways that might persuade the British to yield to them.

Another messenger from Lord North used a chess game to disguise his errand. Lord Howe, an admiral in the British navy and a member of Parliament, arranged for Franklin to be invited to play chess with his sister. After Franklin had played several games with her, Miss Howe said, "What is to be done with this dispute between Great Britain and the colonies? I hope we are not to have a civil war."

"They should kiss and be friends," said Franklin. "What can they do better? Quarreling can be of service to neither, but in ruin to both."

"I have often said," replied Miss Howe, "that I wished

government would employ you to settle the dispute for 'em. I am sure nobody could do it so well. Do you not think that the thing is practicable?"

"Undoubtedly, madam," said Franklin, "if the parties are disposed to reconciliation; for the two countries have really no clashing interests to differ about. 'Tis rather a matter of punctilio which two or three reasonable people might settle in half an hour."

He thanked Miss Howe for her good opinion of him as a peacemaker. "But the ministers will never think of employing me in that good work, they choose rather to abuse me."

"Ay," said Miss Howe, "they have behaved shamefully to you. And indeed some of them are now ashamed of it themselves."

The next time Franklin and Miss Howe met, she introduced her brother to him. Lord Howe soon made it clear that he was hoping to persuade Franklin to join him as a fellow commissioner, appointed by the Crown, to go to America and negotiate a truce. He hinted that if Franklin agreed, he could be sure of receiving every reward that the Crown of England had in its power to confer. Lord Howe was telling Franklin that he could win a knighthood or a baronetcy, and become a very rich man.

Franklin declined to sell out the rights of his country; he insisted on standing behind all America's claims. As he saw it now, Parliament had no right to tax Americans, or rule over them in any way. The only link between England and America was allegiance to the King. This, Americans might be willing to concede, if England gave them the right to rule themselves in every other way. Almost a hundred years later, England realized that Franklin was right, and granted this kind of independence to Canada, Australia and her other overseas dominions. But at this point in history, England refused to give up Parliament's claims.

In the midst of these negotiations Franklin received very bad news from home. His wife Deborah had died. He felt guilty about not having gone home sooner, and immediately prepared to leave. The negotiations to prevent the war dwindled away, as Parliament rejected several proposals by leading members of the opposition to make peace with America. Finally, Franklin's two Quaker friends came to him and told him that he was wasting his time negotiating, and might as well depart. Whatever "pretenses" were offered by the government, "they are all hollow . . . To get a larger field on which to fatten a herd of worthless parasites is all that is regarded."

War was very close, and Franklin knew it. The thought filled him with dread. Already he sensed, on the other side of the world, that his son William disagreed with him on the great political question of America's independence. On his last day in London, Franklin spent some time with an English friend, going over bundles of newspapers recently arrived from America. Franklin pointed out articles that might do America some good, if they were reprinted in English papers "He was frequently not able to proceed for the tears literally running down his cheeks," the friend said later.

CHAPTER 15

DIVIDED FAMILY

ABOARD THE PENNSYLVANIA PACKET, BOUND FOR
Philadelphia, Franklin took with him a young man
named William Temple Franklin, William's illegitimate son.
Throughout his years in England, Franklin had remained close
to the boy, bringing him to Craven Street regularly for visits,
and paying for his education at a good boarding school. Now he
was 16, a handsome, intelligent young man with a gift for
drawing and languages. Franklin did not expect to return to
England, so he was taking Temple home with him.

The sea was calm, the voyage slow. Franklin spent much of
his time writing the longest letter of his life. It began with
those familiar words, "Dear Son," and it continued for 97
pages telling in detail the story of Franklin's secret negotiations with the British government. There was no better proof

of Franklin's anxious desire to prove to William that America was right, and Britain was wrong.

When he was not writing, Franklin found time to investigate further the Gulf Stream, that great ocean river he had noticed on his first voyage back from England. Now he studied it much more carefully, dropping thermometers over the side of the ship, and pulling up samples of the water, which was bright with phosphoresence. He soon decided that a ship sailing from America to Europe could considerably increase its speed by using the Gulf Stream, since the current ran swiftly in that direction. Going from Europe to America, a ship could save days, even weeks, of sailing by avoiding the Stream. But Franklin decided to keep this discovery a secret, for the time being, because, if war broke out, it would be useful primarily to the English, who would be sending dozens of warships to America.

Upon Franklin's arrival in Philadelphia on May 5th, 1775, excited Americans swarmed aboard the ship to inform him that war had begun. Sixteen days before, the British had sent a military expedition to Concord, Massachusetts, to seize cannon, gunpowder and other supplies stored there. Fighting had broken out on the Lexington green at dawn on April 19th, and before the day was over 49 Americans were dead, 41 wounded, and 5 missing. The British retreated from Concord, pursued by hundreds of American Minutemen. Their casualties were 73 killed, 174 wounded and 26 missing. Immediately, Franklin asked the biggest question in his mind: Had William resigned? The answer was no. William felt "obliged" to the British government because they had not removed him from office, in spite of their anger at his father. Governor Franklin felt that both the Americans and the British were partly right and partly wrong. We do not know whether Franklin saw William as soon as he landed in Philadelphia, or if he had a letter from him. We do have a letter that Franklin wrote to him on May 7th, 1775, in which he told his son bluntly where he stood. "I don't understand it as any favour to me or to you, the being continued in an office by which, with all your prudence, you cannot avoid running behindhand, if you live suitably to your station. While you are in it I know you will execute it with fidelity to your master, but I think independence more honourable than any service, and that in the state of American affairs . . . you will find yourself in no uncomfortable situation, and perhaps wish you had soon disengaged yourself."

Franklin was urging William to resign and to join the growing revolution. But neither William, nor Joseph Galloway, Franklin's chief political lieutenant in Pennsylvania, agreed with him. Galloway had proposed a plan of union between England and America and the Continental Congress had voted it down. Declaring himself insulted, he had quit the Congress and gone home.

On May 10, a second Continental Congress met in Philadelphia. Franklin was appointed an extra member of the Pennsylvania delegation. He told everyone that he was for independence, and was stunned to discover that very few people agreed with him. Among these few was a young, lanky delegate from Virginia, Thomas Jefferson. Almost everyone else agreed with John Dickinson, the leader of the Pennsylvania delegation, who was determined to work out a way to reconcile England and America. Franklin had tried this in London, and knew it was a waste of time. But he could only keep silence in Congress, and accept the majority opinion for the time being.

Then came the shocking news of Bunker Hill. The Americans had seized high ground north of Boston, and the British army had attacked them. A tremendous battle erupted, leaving over a thousand British, amd more than 400 Americans, dead and wounded. The village of Charlestown, just below Bunker Hill, was set on fire by cannon balls from British warships, and over 300 houses were destroyed. The news set Franklin's Massachusetts blood boiling. He went home and wrote a scorching letter to his friend, William Strahan.

Philada July 5, 1775

Mr. Strahan,

You are a Member of Parliament, and one of that Majority which has doomed my Country to Destruction.—You have begun to burn our Towns, and murder our People.—Look upon your Hands!—You and I were long Friends:—You are now my Enemy,—and I am

Yours,

B. FRANKLIN

After he wrote the letter, Franklin decided not to mail it. But he realized its value as propaganda, and had it reprinted widely in newspapers.

In spite of his all-out support for the American cause, some people suspected that Franklin was a British spy. A large part of the reason was his son's refusal to join the revolution. The long years Franklin had spent in England, and his friendship with so many powerful men in Parliament, were other reasons why he was suspect. William Bradford, nephew of Franklin's old newspaper competitor, eagerly spread this slander. Richard Henry Lee of Virginia, one of the leading members of the Continental Congress, announced he was launching an investigation to find out if Franklin really was a traitor.

Even more dismaying to Franklin was the decision in Congress to accept John Dickinson's advice and submit another "humble petition" to the king. Called the "Olive Branch Petition," it was written by Dickinson with some help from Thomas Jefferson, and sent to London, in spite of the bloody news from Bunker Hill.

Franklin, totally convinced now that independence was the only solution, wrote a Declaration of Independence and Articles of Confederation, creating an American nation. But when he showed it to the delegates, they were, in Jefferson's words, "revolted at it." Congress was still convinced, in this summer of 1775, that war could somehow be avoided. Politically isolated, Franklin was reduced to uncharacteristic silence in the Continental Congress.

Meanwhile, he worried about his son William and his grandson William Temple. The boy was spending the summer with his father and stepmother in Perth Amboy, New Jersey, and was enjoying himself immensely. Governor Franklin apparently found no difficulty inducing his wife Elizabeth to welcome Temple as a son. The motherless boy had responded with deep affection, and was soon enjoying the lively, well-to-do society that clustered around the Governor in his handsome house.

Most of these people were like William, loyal to the King. Franklin was worried about the effect these people might have on Temple's young mind. He sent the young man many letters, urging him to continue his studies and sending him news from Philadelphia. He told him about Sally's children, who now numbered three. Will, the second one, "has got a little gun, marches with it and whistles at the same time by way of fife," Franklin wrote. He was really telling Temple that even toddlers were aware that war was brewing.

In other letters, Franklin discussed Temple's future with William. They finally decided to enroll the young man in the college at Philadelphia in the fall. William asked his father whether he should bring Temple back to Philadelphia, or would Franklin prefer to come to Perth Amboy to collect him?

With congressmen such as John Adams already talking about arresting Loyalists, the sight of William in Philadelphia would only make Franklin's political influence in Congress even smaller than it already was. He told William that he preferred to come to Perth Amboy.

On this visit, Franklin made one last try to persuade William to join the American side. But William did not think the Americans could win the war. He also did not believe that, if they achieved independence, they could govern themselves. Basically, William did not like America and Americans as much as he liked England and her people. Because of his illegitimate birth, he had never been really accepted in America, while in London (where this fact was unknown), he had been accepted and rewarded with a high government post. He did not share his father's faith in the future of America because he had not found his opportunity, his career in America.

Also there was still for William the golden gleam of the Ohio colony, and he could not help resenting the part his father had played in wrecking this dream. A few weeks after Franklin returned to Philadelphia with Temple, William wrote him a very significant letter. He pointed out that the English partners in the Ohio Company said they had received "the *strongest assurances* that as soon as the present great dispute is settled *our grant shall be perfected.*" William did his own underlining, hinting strongly to his father that Benjamin ought to work for a compromise and stop agitating for independence.

This dispute with his son made Franklin wish that war could be avoided, somehow. He journeyed to Cambridge, Massachusetts, with two other members of Congress, to confer with George Washington, who had taken command of the American army that was besieging the British in Boston.

From there, he wrote to his son-in-law Richard Bache, admitting that he wished "most earnestly for peace, this war being a truly unnatural and mischievous one."

Then William Franklin made a move that almost altered the course of the Revolution. Summoning the New Jersey Assembly, he made a speech to them about "the present unhappy situation of publick affairs." He urged the Assembly to accept the invitation of the British government and petition the King to settle the dispute. Lord North, the British First Minister, had announced in Parliament that they were ready to settle any and all disputes, if each colony petitioned the King separately. Actually the British were hoping to divide and conquer the Americans by breaking the united front they were maintaining in the Continental Congress.

William went on to tell the New Jersey Assemblymen that he was well aware that "sentiments of independency are . . . openly avowed." He called independence a "horrid measure" and asked the Assembly to pass a resolution forbidding the New Jersey delegates in the Continental Congress to vote for it. The Assembly agreed to both of Governor Franklin's requests.

In Philadelphia, the Continental Congress reacted with shock and alarm. If New Jersey's petition reached the King, and he responded with generous grants of money and other favors, more colonies might be tempted to repeat the performance, and American unity would become a "rope of sand." Congress resolved unanimously "that in the present situation of affairs, it will be very dangerous to the liberties and welfare of America, if any colony should separately petition the King or either house of Parliament." They then appointed a committee of three men, and ordered them to rush to Burlington, where the New Jersey Assembly was meeting, to inform the members of this resolution.

After listening to the three congressmen, the Assembly decided to delay their petition until they saw how the King replied to the so-called "Olive Branch Petition."

While his son was trying to wreck the Revolution, Franklin was working harder than ever to make it succeed. Each morning, he arose at 6 a.m. and went to a meeting of the Committee of Safety for the state of Pennsylvania. He bought powder and conferred on the manufacture of guns and cannon. He gave advice on how to block the Delaware River with underwater barriers made of logs and iron, so British warships could not sail up it and bombard Philadelphia.

At 9 o'clock, Franklin trudged to Congress, which was meeting in the Pennsylvania State House. There he served on no less than ten different committees, in addition to his duties as America's first Postmaster General. He had to worry about conciliating the Indians of the "Middle Department" along Pennsylvania's and Virginia's borders, advise Congress on ways to protect the trade of the colonies, and confer with generals and engineers on supplying and equipping the American army.

By far the most important committee on which Franklin

served began its work during the same month of December, 1775, that saw William Franklin's attempt to thwart the Revolution. The elder Franklin and four other congressmen were appointed to a secret committee with "the sole purpose of corresponding with our friends in Great Britain, Ireland and other parts of the world."

A few days later, the French-born librarian of the Philadelphia Library introduced Franklin to an "Antwerp merchant" who had come to America "out of curiosity." The man was actually a French spy, sent by the French government to see how the American Revolution was progressing. Franklin and his fellow committee members met with this man several times during the month of December. They maintained the strictest secrecy about these meetings. Each time they met, they chose a different building, and each member of the committee traveled alone, by a different route. The French secret agent assured them that "France wished them well," but he hesitated to say that France was ready to support the Americans. "It was slippery business in the face of the English," he said. He agreed to help the Americans hire French military engineers, and buy muskets and ammunition in France.

On January 2nd, 1776, Congress passed a resolution calling on local authorities in the various colonies to restrain the "wicked practices" of those "unworthy Americans" who persisted in supporting the [Royal government.] Within three days, the commander of the American army in New Jersey arrested Governor William Franklin. He intercepted letters that William had sent to the British government, identifying all the leaders of the Revolution in New Jersey, and discussing the rebellion in detail. The Congress, embarrassed by the fact that he was Benjamin Franklin's son, decided to let William remain in his house; and New Jersey continued to pay his salary as Royal Governor.

William tried to win Temple's sympathy by writing a letter describing the rough way that the army had surrounded his house with bayonet-wielding soldiers at 2 o'clock in the morning. Elizabeth Franklin had been so frightened, the Governor was certain that "another alarm of the like nature will put an end to her life." William reminded Temple how affectionately Mrs. Franklin had accepted him as her stepson. "Let what will happen, I hope you will never be wanting in a grateful sense of her kindness to you," he said.

Temple was deeply disturbed by his father's letter, and wrote an immediate answer, full of apologies and sympathy. But Benjamin Franklin did not communicate with his stubborn son. He had done everything in his power to convince him to change sides before it was too late. Now William would have to take the consequences for his decision.

CHAPTER 16

HANGING TOGETHER — OR SEPARATELY

IN THE EARLY MONTHS OF 1776, MORE AND MORE Americans began to realize that Franklin was right— independence was America's only hope. The King had declared the colonies in revolt and outside his protection, forbade all nations to trade with them and authorized the seizure of American ships on the high seas.

Meanwhile, a close Franklin friend, Thomas Paine, published on January 10th, 1776, a two-shilling pamphlet of 47 pages called "Common Sense." It was a devastating attack on the two ideas that still prevented most Americans from voting for independence loyalty to the King, and the British Constitution. The pamphlet was a sensational success—in less than three months, 120,000 copies were sold. Many people thought

Franklin had written it, and, indeed, Paine may have gotten many of his ideas for it from talking with Franklin, who had written letters of introduction for him when he emigrated to America from England in 1774. Paine gave Franklin the first copy of the pamphlet that came off the press.

On March 3rd, Franklin's committee sent a secret agent of their own to France. He was Silas Deane, a Connecticut merchant. Franklin gave him introductions to many of his friends in France, and wrote a long letter, carefully instructing Deane on how to deal with the French foreign Minister, Count de Vergennes.

A few weeks later, Congress called on Franklin to take an exhausting trip to Canada. An American army was attempting to bring that colony into the revolutionary confederation, but the British army there had counterattacked and seemed on the point of driving the Americans out of the colony. Franklin traveled up Lake George and Lake Champlain in open boats, through water thick with ice. The weather was bitterly cold, and he bought a fur hat to keep his balding head warm. Between the terrible weather and the long journey, Franklin thought at one point he was dying, and wrote letters of farewell to several friends.

In Canada, he found that the American army was disintegrating because they had no money. He turned around and struggled back down the lakes to New York. On his return journey, his legs swelled, and boils broke out all over his body. He might well have died, except for the help he received from

Father John Carroll, an American priest who had voluntarily joined the American mission, in the hope of persuading the Catholic French Canadians to side with the Americans. But the Catholic Bishop of Quebec preferred to stick with the British, and Father Carroll, seeing that he was wasting his time in Canada and realizing the seriousness of Franklin's condition, had offered to make the journey home with him. From New York, Franklin wrote friends in Albany, "I think I could hardly have got along so far, but for Mister Carroll's friendly assistance and tender care of me."

In New York, Franklin felt well enough to have tea with an old friend named Mrs. Barrow. Her husband had joined the Loyalists aboard the British ships in the harbor. Franklin had paid her a visit on his way to Canada, and she had told him she feared that the American soldiers in New York might abuse her, because of her husband's politics. Franklin had gone directly to George Washington, and made sure that she would not be molested. At tea, he asked "how our people had behaved" to her. She told him that everyone had treated her with the utmost decorum and respect.

"I'm glad of that," said Franklin. "Why if they had used you ill I would have turned Tory."

"In that case," she said, with a twinkle in her eye, "I wish they had."

Back in Philadelphia, Franklin found that his son William was still against the Revolution. On May 15th, 1776, Congress had passed a resolution abolishing all "oaths and affirmations" to the Crown of Great Britain, and called on Americans to suppress all aspects of Royal authority that remained in the colonies. Ignoring this clear warning, Governor William Franklin issued a call for the New Jersey Assembly to meet in Perth Amboy on June 20th.

Unfortunately for William, the Third Provincial Congress of New Jersey—the local revolutionary government—was already in session, and decided that William's call was "in direct contempt and violation of the resolve of the Continental Congress." The members declared that William was "an enemy of the liberties of this country" and ordered him arrested, and his salary as Royal Governor "from henceforth to cease." At the same time, they urged the arresting officers to conduct themselves "with all the delicacy and tenderness which the nature of the business could possibly admit." If Governor Franklin agreed to sign a parole guaranteeing his good conduct, he would be permitted to live unmolested on his farm at Rancocas Creek below Burlington.

But Governor Franklin was totally uncooperative. He defied the soldiers who arrested him, and told the committee of the Provincial Congress who examined him that they could "do as you please and make the best of it." The committeemen informed the Continental Congress that William was "a virulent enemy to this country." On Monday, June 24th, the Continental Congress resolved that "William Franklin be sent under guard to Governor Trumbull of [Connecticut]."

William Franklin, still fighting for Temple's allegiance, wrote a bitter letter to his son, describing his ordeal. He called the New Jersey committeemen "low mightinesses" and described how they ordered him to make the trip to Connecticut, in spite of his claim that he was too sick to travel. "Hypocrites always suspect hypocrisy in others," the Governor said. Then, shifting gears, he urged Temple "to be dutiful and attentive to your grandfather" and "love Mrs. Franklin for she loves you, and will do all she can for you if I should never return more."

Throughout the last two weeks in June, Benjamin Franklin used his weakened condition, a result of his trip to Canada, as a good excuse to avoid attending Congress. He took little or no part in the fight to pass a declaration of independence. Congress appointed him a member of the committee to prepare this document. As the most famous man in Congress, and a writer with a world-wide reputation, Franklin would seem to have been the logical man to write the Declaration. But the embarrassment of his Tory son cast a shadow over his appeal as a Revolutionary spokesman. So the committee members gave the job to 33-year-old Thomas Jefferson, who was from Virginia, the largest of the 13 colonies, and a delegate without political liabilities.

Franklin made only a few minor changes in the wording of Jefferson's great document. Perhaps the most important was where Jefferson had written "We hold these truths to be sacred and undeniable" Franklin crossed out "sacred and undeniable" and substituted "self-evident."

Franklin roused himself and came to Congress to vote in

favor of independence on July 2nd. He sat next to Jefferson, on the following day, as Congress went over the Declaration and deleted several sections of it. Jefferson was very disappointed and annoyed by this surgery. When it was over, and the final shortened version had won a vote of approval, Franklin tried to cheer Jefferson up. "I have made it a rule," he said, "whenever in my power to avoid becoming the draftsman of papers to be reviewed by a public body." To explain why, Franklin told Jefferson a story from his journeyman printer days. One of his friends, an apprentice hatter, decided to open a shop for himself. "His first concern was to have a handsome signboard with a proper inscription. He composed it in these words: *John Thompson, hatter, makes and sells hats for ready money,* with a figure of a hat subjoined. But he thought he would submit it to his friends for their amendments."

The first man he showed it to thought the word "hatter" was superfluous because it was followed by the words "makes hats." Thompson agreed and struck it out. The next friend observed that the word "makes" might as well be omitted, because the customers would not care who made the hats, as long as they were good ones. Thompson agreed and struck it out. A third friend suggested eliminating "for ready money" because none of the local merchants sold on credit. Again Thompson bowed to the will of the majority, and now he had a sign which said: "John Thompson sells hats."

"Sells hats," said his next friend, "why nobody will expect you to give them away. What then is the use of that word?"

Again poor Thompson conceded. Moments later, the word "hats" went into oblivion when another friend pointed out that there was one painted on the board. And so he was left with a sign that said "John Thompson" beneath the painted hat.

It was like Franklin to tell a joke at the moment when he was voting for the Declaration that would make him a traitor, liable to be hanged, drawn and quartered under English law. Contrary to the myth, no one actually signed the Declaration on July 4th. Not until August 2nd was a final copy engrossed on parchment and signed by the members of the Congress. Then, Franklin reportedly told another joke. John Hancock, after placing his large scrawl at the head of the list of signers, as befitted the President of Congress, said, "We must be unanimous, there must be no pulling different ways; we must all hang together."

"Yes," Franklin replied, "we must indeed all hang together, or most assuredly we shall all hang separately."

When Franklin had written his own Declaration of Independence, in the summer of 1775, he had attached to it Articles of Confederation. Now he threw all his energy into persuading Congress to form a union as quickly as possible. But he could not get them to agree. The smaller states demanded an equal vote with the large states. Of course, they did not have as many men or as much money to contribute to the war effort. Franklin warned them that having "an equal vote without bearing equal burdens" meant that the confederation would

129

"never last long." The smaller colonies replied that they were afraid the larger colonies would reduce them to "vassals." The weather was hot, and the arguments were ever hotter. Franklin tried to cool everyone off with a joke.

He told them a story he had heard in England about the opposition of Scottish peers to the union between England and Scotland. One nobleman predicted "that as the whale had swallowed Jonah, so Scotland would be swallowed by England." But there were soon so many Scotsmen in high places in the English government that it looked like "Jonah had swallowed the whale." An admiring Jefferson later recalled, "This little story produced a general laugh and restored good humour." But neither humor nor reason could persuade the large state and small state men to agree.

Meanwhile, the British were massing a huge army on Staten Island, and preparing to attack George Washington and his largely amateur soldiers, who were entrenched on Long Island and in New York. On August 27th, the British attacked the Americans on Long Island, and beat them badly. Only a near miraculous combination of good luck, British overconfidence and foggy weather enabled Washington to escape by night with most of his army to Manhattan Island.

Lord Howe, the British admiral who had tried to negotiate with Franklin in London, appeared in New York harbor as commander in chief of the British navy. He said he had a commission from the King, to negotiate peace. Franklin and two other congressmen met with Lord Howe on Staten Island, but the conference ended in failure, because Lord Howe only had power to issue pardons, if and when Americans made their "submission" to the King. Franklin told him that Americans did not feel they had done anything that needed pardoning. He also told him that independence was now an unchangeable fact, and Britain had better face it, and negotiate with Americans as a separate country.

The British reply was a new attack on Washington's army. They stormed ashore at Kips Bay in Manhattan, and routed the raw American recruits who were supposed to be protecting this landing place. The American army fled, leaving George Washington alone on the battlefield. More and more, it began to look as if William Franklin was right in his opinion that the Americans could not hope to defeat Britain's professional army and navy.

From France, around this time, came more bad news. Franklin's friends wrote him, assuring him that the French government and the French people were sympathetic to the American cause, but despairing that none of the King's ministers "will espouse it with warmth." France was "over head and ears in debt." Congress, terribly alarmed by American defeats, decided that an alliance with France was an absolute necessity. They had heard nothing from Silas Deane, the secret agent Franklin's committee had sent to France in March. So they decided to send a more impressive ambassador— Benjamin Franklin.

This decision meant that Franklin would have to endure a

winter voyage across the Atlantic. At his age, this might in itself be a death sentence. An additional danger were the British cruisers which swarmed the ocean, for if one captured him on such a mission, a traitor's death at the end of a hangman's rope in London would be a certainty. But Franklin was totally committed to the Revolution. Turning to young Dr. Benjamin Rush of Philadelphia, who sat next to him in Congress, Franklin said, "I am old and good for nothing; but, as the storekeepers say of their remnants of cloth, 'I am but a fag end, and you may have me for what you please,' just so my country may command my services in any way they choose."

Franklin's first thoughts as he planned the voyage were of William Temple Franklin, now staying with his stepmother in New Jersey. Already, the boy had written his grandfather an angry letter when Franklin had refused to let him take a trip to visit his father in Wallingford, Connecticut, where Governor Franklin was being held a prisoner. If he left Temple behind in America, the boy would almost certainly become a Loyalist. So Franklin decided to take Temple with him. Quickly, he rushed a note to him in New Jersey, urging him to return to Philadelphia immediately. "I hope . . . that your mother will make no objection to it, something offering here that will be much to your advantage if you are not out of the way."

Franklin also decided to take with him his six-year-old grandson Benjamin Franklin Bache. The war was disrupting schools in America, and Franklin wanted the boy to get the best possible education. So, with his two young friends for company, Franklin rode to Marcus Hook on the Delaware, where boats took them aboard the American sloop *Reprisal*.

Franklin's faith in America's future remained amazingly strong. The day before he sailed, he wrote to a friend in Boston, "I hope our people will keep up their courage. I have no doubt of their finally succeeding by the blessing of God, nor have I any doubt that so good a cause will fail of that blessing."

CHAPTER 17

EXTRAORDINARY DIPLOMAT

THE VOYAGE IN THE *REPRISAL* WAS A TERRIBLE ordeal. The seas were turbulent, with mountainous waves, and the weather bitterly cold. There was nothing to eat but salt beef and ship's biscuits. Franklin wore the fur hat he had acquired in Canada, but it did little good. The boils that had tormented him in Canada broke out again, and he felt himself growing more and more feeble. His only consolation was the speed that the ship was making.

One day toward the end of the fourth week, the captain of the *Reprisal,* Lambert Wickes, burst into Franklin's cabin and asked for permission to attack a British ship. Wickes had received orders from Congress to avoid all encounters with the enemy until he had deposited Franklin safely in France. But now they were close to the French shore, and the ship, a plodding merchantman, was a tempting plum. Franklin took one look, and nodded his permission. The crew of the *Reprisal* raced to quarters, and the British ship surrendered without a shot. A prize crew was swiftly put aboard her. A few hours later, Wickes repeated the performance with another British ship. Franklin was delighted to see Americans strike a blow at England in her home waters.

Six days later, the *Reprisal* anchored off Brittany, near the small fishing village of Auray. Franklin was so exhausted he could barely stand, but he immediately fired off a letter to Silas Deane in Paris. "I am weak, but hope the good air which I breathe on land will soon re-establish me," he said. It took 24 hours to find a carriage and two tired horses in a neighboring town, but finally Franklin and his two grandsons started down the road to the port of Nantes.

After resting in Nantes, Franklin joined Deane in Paris. He enrolled young Benjamin Franklin Bache in a local private school, where he was soon speaking French like a native. In fact, the boy learned the language so well, he almost forgot how to speak English. Franklin and William Temple Franklin moved into the Hotel de Hambourg with Silas Deane and the two men went to work.

Franklin was pleased to learn that the French government had set up a dummy company, and had loaned the Americans two million livres—about $400,000—to buy guns and supplies. Some ships had already sailed. But when the French heard the bad news about Washington's defeats on Long Island and around New York, they refused to permit other ships to sail, in spite of the fact that they were already loaded and ready to depart.

This made Deane and his assistant, a Marylander named William Carmichael, very angry with France. But Franklin understood why the French were cautious—England had beaten them very badly in the last war, and they had no desire to suffer another defeat. Before they publicly supported the United States, they wanted to make sure the Americans could fight.

In Paris, Franklin continued to wear his fur hat, which caused a great deal of comment among the fashion conscious French. They liked it. They saw it as proof that Americans were simple and honest, and did not bother with trivial matters, such as wearing the right wig, or the latest fashion in hats. Franklin also made a point of wearing very plain brown or black suits, and white shirts. One Frenchman vowed that everything about him typified "simplicity and innocence."

Franklin was neither simple nor innocent, but he recognized the importance of winning the French people to his side. So he continued to wear his fur hat. With the help of Jacques Chaumont, a French businessman who was working with Silas Deane to supply the American army, Franklin had a painting of himself wearing the fur hat printed on plates, pitchers and other pieces of crockery, which were produced by the thousands in ovens at Chaumont's estate. They sold at a tremendous rate, and Franklin was soon able to remark that his face was better known in France than the face of the man in the moon.

At the same time, Franklin coped shrewdly with British attempts to wreck his mission. When an American woman living in France warned him that he was surrounded by British spies, he replied that he had "no doubt" this was true. In fact, he said that if he were sure that his valet was a spy, "as probably he is, I think I should not discharge him for that, if in other respects I lik'd him." Franklin saw that it would be to his advantage if the British learned about French secret aid, for this might make them so angry that they would declare war on France. It did not particularly matter to him just how France became America's ally. In fact, one of Franklin's closest aides in Paris, Connecticut-born Edward Bancroft, was a double agent who took 600 pounds a year from the British Secret Service and reported everything Franklin was doing to George III.

The British did become very angry at the sight of Franklin in Paris. The British ambassador, Lord Stormont, protested violently to the French government. The British newspapers were filled with stories claiming that Franklin had fled to France to save his skin, because the Revolution was collapsing. In a letter to his young friend Polly Stevenson Hewson, who was still in England, Franklin wrote, "I must contrive to get you to America. I want all my friends out of that wicked country. I have just seen in the papers seven paragraphs about me, of which six were lies."

In March, 1777, Franklin moved out of the Hotel de Hambourg and retreated to the village of Passy, about a half hour's drive from Paris on the road to Versailles, the palace of Louis XVI and the center of the French government. He accepted the invitation of the Chaumonts to live rent free in one of the houses on their estate, the Hôtel de Valentinois.

Franklin was soon asking the French Foreign Minister, Count Vergennes, to come to America's aid with a formal alliance. But Vergennes was still not sure that the Americans could win the war. The news from the battlefields in America continued to be bad. Washington had won small victories at Trenton and Princeton, but the latest word indicated that the British were mustering all their strength to deliver a knockout blow. One British army, commanded by General John Burgoyne, was to invade the colonies from Canada, while the main army, based in New York, would attack Philadelphia. So Count Vergennes stalled, offering Franklin more secret aid, but declining to become a public ally.

Calmly, Franklin asked Vergennes if there was any objection against Captain Lambert Wickes doing a little cruising against British vessels, and bringing his prizes into French ports. Vergennes reluctantly replied that there was no objection if Wickes' ship was "a vessel in distress." As for the prizes, that would depend on how loudly the British yelled. Under Franklin's orders, Captain Wickes promptly stood out of Nantes and in a matter of days picked off four British merchantmen. Next, he captured the Royal mail packet to Lisbon, the H.M.S. *Swallow*. Then he opened his seacocks until there was enough water in his hold to prove his "distress" and sailed his prizes back into Nantes.

The British Ambassador Lord Stormont protested wildly. Vergennes cooled him off by ordering Wickes and his prizes out of French waters within 24 hours. Of course, by this time all the prizes had been sold, taken offshore and hastily repainted, and their cargoes transferred to other ships. Meanwhile, Franklin sent Wickes orders to make another raid in British waters before he returned to America.

At the same time, Franklin launched another tough sailor, Gustavus Conyngham, a hotheaded daredevil from County Donegal, to war on British shipping. On May 3rd, Conyngham captured the British mail packet *The Prince of Orange* loaded with confidential documents the government was sending to its ambassadors in Europe. The documents were full of lies about the coming collapse of the Revolution, and Franklin cheerfully published them, with his refutations.

This time Lord Stormont almost went berserk. He demanded the arrest of Conyngham and his crew as pirates. Vergennes, still trying to avoid a break with England, arrested them, but declined to surrender them to the British. With the aid of the captured documents, and his native wit, Franklin was able to make a fool of Lord Stormont. One day a French friend rushed to Franklin to repeat the latest story about America's collapse, which he had heard from the British ambassador. Six battalions in Washington's army had laid down their arms. Was it true? "Oh, no," replied Franklin gravely, "it is not the truth, it is only a Stormont." Within a day the story had swept Paris, and *stormonter* became a new French word for lying. Lord Stormont was so upset, one day he wrote no less than nine letters to London about Franklin's activities.

Around this time, Franklin found himself dining at the same inn as Edward Gibbon, the famous author of *The Decline and Fall of the Roman Empire*. Gibbon, a fat, nearsighted little man, was a member of Parliament who voted blindly in support of the government's policies. Franklin invited Gibbon to join him at his table, but the historian primly replied that a servant of the King could not have any conversation with a rebel. Franklin sent back his regrets—and then could not resist adding that if Mr. Gibbon ever decided to write a book on the decline and fall of the British Empire, he would be happy to supply him with "ample materials."

Then came more bad news from America. Burgoyne had captured Fort Ticonderoga, the key defense point on America's northern frontier; and Washington had been defeated by the British at the battle of Brandywine, near Philadelphia. In addition, many of the supply ships which Deane had sent had been captured by blockading British warships. Obviously, America was in desperate need of French support.

Franklin also received some very bad news of a more personal kind from America during this gloomy fall of 1777.

William Franklin had been caught signing and smuggling out of Connecticut official pardons which the British were using in New Jersey and had been thrown into the town jail in Litchfield, Connecticut. Meanwhile, the British army abandoned New Jersey and took William's wife Elizabeth with them. In New York, without funds or friends, Elizabeth soon fell ill, and died. Temple Franklin was very sad when he heard this news, for she was the only mother he had ever known. He could not help remembering the words his father had written to him, urging him to take care of her. Temple was torn between his desire to be loyal to his grandfather and to America, and his love for his father and stepmother. It had a bad effect on Temple, emotionally. He became very cynical, and tried to tell himself that love did not matter. He swore he would never marry, because marriage only produced unhappiness.

Franklin had little time to console William. The barrage of bad news from America continued, and this time it was bad news both for America and for Franklin. The British had captured Philadelphia. All Franklin's property and, as far as he knew, his beloved daughter and her children were in the hands of the enemy. He had to struggle to keep up a brave front when Frenchmen asked him what was happening to the American Cause. "Well, Doctor," one Parisian said to him, "Howe has taken Philadelphia."

"I beg your pardon, sir," said Franklin, "Philadelphia has taken Howe."

Less than a week after this dismal news, a rumor came

drifting into Paris from Nantes. An American ship had arrived with a messenger carrying official dispatches for Franklin and his associates. The Americans and their French friends gathered at Franklin's house at Passy to await the arrival of the courier.

The moment a carriage was heard rattling over the cobblestones of the courtyard, Franklin and the others rushed out of the house. Jonathan Loring Austin of Boston got out. "Sir," Franklin asked, "is Philadelphia taken?"

"Yes, sir," replied Austin.

Franklin nodded mournfully. He had been hoping that the story was another British lie. Then, as he turned away, young Austin spoke again. "But, sir, I have greater news than that. General Burgoyne and his whole army are prisoners of war!"

It was true. New England militiamen, armed in many cases with guns from a ship sent by Silas Deane which had broken through the British blockade, had trapped Burgoyne's army near Saratoga, and he had surrendered.

Franklin immediately rushed into the house and began writing dispatches and letters. Some went to friends in England, to give the opposition in Parliament ammunition against the Ministry. Other letters went to friends in Paris. The most important one went to Count Vergennes, the French Foreign Minister, urging an alliance between France and America. To make sure everyone in Paris heard the news, Franklin had printed in French a handbill telling the story, newspaper style.

"Mail arrived from Philadelphia at Dr. Franklin's home in Passy after 34 days.

"On October 14th, Burgoyne had to lay down his arms, 9200 men killed or taken prisoner. . . ."

Vergennes said he was now ready to sign a treaty of alliance. But first he needed the approval of Spain. The Spanish King was an ally, as well as a Bourbon relative, of France's King, Louis XVI. When Spain refused to sign the treaty, the alliance was threatened with more—possibly fatal—delay. Franklin proceeded to have dinner with the head of the British Secret Service in Paris, whereupon the French became vastly alarmed. They were afraid that he was thinking about signing a truce with England. They did not know, of course, what Franklin said to the spy at dinner. England, the spy told Franklin, was ready to fight ten years to prevent America from winning independence. America, Franklin shot back, was ready to fight sixty years to win it.

The French now practically implored Franklin to sign a treaty of alliance. He was reluctant to do so, because he knew that it would mean a longer and more bitter war. He waited until the last possible moment, hoping to hear from England that the opposition had brought down the government and a pro-American Ministry had taken power. To Thomas Walpole, an old friend from the proposed Ohio Company, he wrote, "Everything seems to be rejected by your mad politicians that would lead to healing the breach." To another English friend, on February 5th, 1778, he wrote, "Understanding that a certain person promised to make proposals for healing a certain breach, I postponed and delay'd a material operation till I shou'd hear what those proposals were. I am now told that he will not make them . . . Therefore, adieu, my dear friend."

The following day, Franklin went to the Ministry of Foreign Affairs and signed the treaty of alliance with France. Friends noticed he wore the same Manchester velvet suit that he had worn the day he had been abused by Wedderburn before the Privy Council. They asked him why. Franklin smiled and said, "To give it a little revenge."

CHAPTER 18

PEACE NEGOTIATOR

THE BRITISH REFUSED TO GIVE UP THE FIGHT, in spite of the French alliance, and the war dragged on. The other Americans who were supposed to be helping Franklin in Paris quarreled with each other, and with him, probably because they envied him his great fame. The chief trouble-maker was a Virginian, Arthur Lee, who suspected everyone of being a traitor, even Franklin. Nothing ever pleased him.

One day, Deane and Lee were dining with Franklin, whose French neighbors had sent in a large cake with the inscription, *Le digne Franklin* (The worthy Franklin).

"As usual, Doctor," Silas Deane said, "we have to appropriate your present to our joint use."

Seeing a sour look on Arthur Lee's face, Franklin said, "Not at all. This must be intended for all the commissioners; only these French people cannot write English. They mean, no doubt, Lee, Deane, Franklin."

"That might answer," growled the humorless Lee, "but we know that whenever they remember us at all, they always put you first."

Eventually, Congress recalled Deane and Lee and gave Franklin the sole responsibility for representing the United States in Paris. This meant a lot more headaches. Franklin had to buy all the guns and other supplies for the American army. He had to be a part-time admiral, and supervise the activity of American warships in European waters. He had to worry about over a thousand American seamen who had been captured and were starving to death in British jails. He had to interview hundreds of officers from France, Germany and other countries who wanted to volunteer to fight in the American army. All these were extra duties, piled on top of his most important job—maintaining harmony between France and America, and persuading the French government to continue to loan money to the bankrupt Americans.

There were times when the European volunteers almost drove Franklin crazy. "Great officers in all ranks, in all departments; ladies great and small . . . worry me from morning to night," he complained. "The noise of every coach now that enters my court terrifies me. I am afraid to accept an invitation to dine abroad, being almost sure of meeting with some officer or officer's friend, who, as soon as I am put in good humour by a glass or two of champaign, begins his attack upon me. . . ."

As usual, Franklin saw the humorous side of the situation. One day he cooked up a "model of a letter of recommendation of a person you are unacquainted with." The letter, which he actually gave to some people going to America, explained that Franklin did not know the person, but he recommended him "to those civilities which every stranger of whom one knows no harm has a right to."

Around this time Franklin heard a story from England that cheered him up. Before the war, George III had permitted Franklin to install lightning rods on St. James Palace in London, where the royal family lived. A British electrician, Benjamin Wilson, told the King that Franklin's pointed lightning conductors were inferior to blunt ones. The King asked Franklin's old friend, Sir John Pringle, the physician to the royal family, for his opinion. Pringle replied that natural laws were not changeable by royal pleasure. George flew into a rage, barred Pringle from the palace, removed him as president of the Royal Society and replaced all the pointed conductors on St. James with blunt ones.

The wrangle inspired the following verse from a London wit.

While you Great George, for safety hunt
And sharp conductors change for blunt
　　The nation's out of joint.
Franklin a wiser course pursues
And all your thunder fearless views
　　By keeping to the *point*.

147

Franklin worried constantly over the American seamen in British jails. Through friends in England, he set up a fund which was supposed to pay them small amounts of money each week so they could buy decent food. The man in charge of this fund was a Maryland merchant, Thomas Digges, who had been selected by Arthur Lee. Unfortunately, Digges was a British agent. He took the 400 pounds—over $2,000—which Franklin sent to England, and instead of passing it on to the prisoners each week, he kept it in his own pocket.

Franklin condemned Digges in a scorching letter. "He that robs the rich even of a single guinea is a villain; but what is he who can break his sacred trust, by robbing a poor man and a prisoner of 18 pence given in charity for his relief and repeat that crime as often as there are weeks in a winter, and multiply it by robbing as many poor men every week as made up the number of near six hundred? We have no name in our language for such atrocious wickedness. If such a fellow is not damned, it is not worthwhile to keep a devil."

A British friend wrote a worried letter to Franklin, because he had heard a rumor that the secret agents of George III were planning to assassinate him. Franklin declined to be frightened by the story. "I thank you for your kind caution," he wrote, "but having nearly finished a long life, I set but little value on what remains of it . . . Perhaps the best use such an old fellow can be put to, is to make a martyr of him." No more was heard of an assassination plot.

At Passy, Franklin became warm friends with all his neighbors. The ladies especially loved him, and called him "mon cher Papa." His two favorites were Madame Brillon, a pretty, very gifted musician of 35, and Madame Helvetius, a widow of over 50, still rather beautiful, the daughter of an aristocrat. Franklin loved to tease Madame Brillon about being in love with her. But she regarded him as her "spiritual father." He finally agreed to adopt her as his "daughter," and in his letters he always called her that. When she had trouble with her husband, Madame Brillon fled to Franklin for advice. She depended on him, exactly as many daughters depend on their fathers.

With Madame Helvetius, Franklin had a different relationship. He actually fell in love with her and proposed marriage. But she said that she wished to remain faithful to the memory of her husband, and refused his offer. Franklin proceeded to write her a little story, in the hope of changing her mind. He said he had dreamt that he had died and gone to heaven, where he met Mr. Helvetius. Gravely, Helvetius informed Franklin that he had taken a new wife in Paradise. At that moment, the wife appeared, and Franklin was amazed to discover it was his wife on earth, Deborah. "Come," he said to Madame Helvetius, "let us revenge ourselves." But Madame still said no.

These loving friends helped to ease Franklin's pain when he heard more depressing news about his son William in America. The Continental Congress finally agreed to exchange William for a captured British general. In New York, William became head of the Board of Associated Loyalists, an organization that recruited men to fight on the British side. They began launching guerrilla raids against Americans loyal to Congress, in New Jersey, on Long Island, and in Connecticut. This hurt Franklin deeply. It was bad enough to have his son refuse to stand by him in the fight for American independence, but now he was fighting against his fellow Americans, in the meanest, cruelest way, killing people from ambush and burning homes and barns. To Franklin it meant that he could never again feel a father's love for William.

Franklin hoped that William Temple Franklin would take William's place. But Temple was emotionally wounded by the decision he had to make between his father and his grandfather. Part of the time he worked for Franklin, but most of the time he preferred to be a playboy, wearing the latest fashions and ogling the girls in Paris. At home in America, Arthur Lee tried to strike at Franklin through Temple, by accusing the young man of being a Loyalist, and possibly a spy. "Is it enough that I have lost my son; would they add my grandson?" Franklin cried in a letter to his son-in-law, Richard Bache. If Congress ordered him to fire Temple as his secretary, Franklin declared, he would quit.

As for his other grandson, Ben Bache, once he had learned French, Franklin sent him to school in Geneva, Switzerland. "He is a good, honest lad and will make, I think, a valuable man," Franklin said. He was right—Ben became a very successful newspaper editor.

Franklin wrote Ben many letters while the boy was in

Geneva. He always urged him to study hard. "I think of you every day," he wrote in one letter, "and there is nothing I desire more than to see you furnished with good learning [so that you can become] an honourable man in your own country."

The war dragged on and on. Then, in the fall of 1781, Franklin got an unexpected letter from Count Vergennes. He thought it might be a complaint, because the Americans were trying to borrow more money from France. Instead the letter contained the best possible news. The Americans had trapped another British army at Yorktown, Virginia, and the best British general in America, Charles Lord Cornwallis, had surrendered to George Washington. Franklin told Vergennes that King Louis XVI was *le plus grand faiseur d'heureux* (the greatest creator of happiness) in the world.

In the spring of 1782, the upheaval in the British Parliament which Franklin had been hoping to see for so many years finally took place. The opposition voted Lord North and his ministers out of power. The new Foreign Minister was William Petty, Lord Shelburne, Franklin's old friend. He immediately sent a personal representative to Franklin, telling him that England wanted peace. Franklin urged Shelburne to do more than negotiate a peace treaty. "Reconcile England and America," he advised him. How? Along with granting the thirteen colonies independence, Franklin said, Shelburne ought to give them as a gift Canada and Nova Scotia. This land could be used to pay for the millions of dollars of damage that England's armies and fleets had done to America's towns and cities. Shelburne's representative at the peace conference, Richard Oswald, agreed completely with this idea. If Franklin had been able to push the negotiations through, alone, America might have won complete control of the North American continent.

But Franklin was not the only peace negotiator on the American side. Two other men had been appointed by Congress, John Jay and John Adams, both lawyers who tended to see everything in legal terms. Jay refused to negotiate with the British until they formally recognized the independence of the United States. Adams sided with Jay, so Franklin was overruled. For over two months the Americans wrangled with the British over this point. During this time, the British won two victories in the war. Their fleet fought a battle in the West Indies with the French fleet, and beat them badly. Spain, which had entered the war late on France's side, tried to capture Gilbraltar with a massive assault. But the Spanish army was beaten off, and a British fleet broke through with supplies. These victories made the British much tougher bargainers at the peace table.

In the end, the Americans were glad to settle for all the territory between the seacoast and the Mississippi River, with boundaries on the north and south about where they are today. Even then, the British were not inclined to sign the treaty until Americans agreed to pay the Loyalists for their farms, estates and houses, which they were forced to abandon in most colonies.

Franklin arose to play a trump card. He read a list of the cities and towns which the British had burned or looted in the course of the war. He went over the thousands of men, women and children slaughtered on the frontier by British-led Indian raids. Before the British talked about compensating the Loyalists, let them pay this bill. The British negotiators swallowed hard, conferred for a moment, and agreed to sign the treaty as it stood.

Franklin was more than satisfied with this victory. He knew that in this world one cannot always win everything. The mere fact that the thirteen colonies had won their independence in spite of all the efforts of Great Britain, the strongest nation on the globe, was almost a miracle.

Less than a month later, the British and the French signed a treaty of peace. The war was over. That night, arriving at the home of a French friend, Franklin threw his arms around him and exclaimed, "Could I have hoped, at my age, to enjoy such a happiness?"

With peace secured, Franklin's spirits soared. He forgave everyone who had ever wronged him. When John Jay wrote from London to tell him that he had many enemies in England, Franklin replied that the fact did not trouble him. "They are my enemies as an *American*." He added that he also had two or three enemies in America "who are my enemies as a minister." But he was able to thank God "there are not in the whole world any who are my enemies as a man; for by His grace, thro' a long life, I have been enabled so to conduct myself, that there does

153

not exist a human being who can justly say 'Ben. Franklin has wrong'd me.' "

When William Strahan wrote to Franklin, lamenting the confused state of English politics, Franklin told him not to despair. "We have some remains of affection for you, and shall always be ready to receive and take care of you in case of distress. So if you have not sense and virtue enough to govern yourselves . . . dissolve your present old crazy Constitution, and send members to Congress."

Soon after, Franklin had an opportunity to repay an old debt of gratitude. In his years at the Court of Versailles he had become very friendly with the Papal Legate, the priest who represented the Pope of Rome in France. The Papal diplomat now informed the Ambassador that America's independence had convinced the Pope that the Catholic Church in America was ready to take an important step toward maturity. It was time to appoint an American bishop. Did he have any suggestions? Franklin had only one—his old friend Father John Carroll, who had saved his life on the trip down the lakes from Canada in 1776. The Papal Legate passed on Franklin's recommendation to Rome, and soon a very surprised Father Carroll was America's first bishop.

Meanwhile, Franklin was enjoying himself with a new scientific interest—balloons. The French had begun filling balloons, first with heated air, then with hydrogen, which Franklin called "inflammable air." To fellow scientists in England and America, Franklin sent detailed reports on these first balloon flights. As with the American trip to the moon, there were numerous pessimists, who bemoaned the expense and time—it took two days and nights to fill a balloon—and demanded to know what was the point of ballooning, what good did it do the average man? Franklin, foreseeing the day when men would be able to fly everywhere, replied: "What good is a newborn baby?"

Franklin's French friends urged him to spend the rest of his life in France. But he decided, somewhat reluctantly, to go home. "I want to die in my own country," he said. He had developed a stone in his bladder, which made riding in a carriage very painful, so the King sent him a litter, drawn by his Royal mules. In this conveyance, Franklin began his journey to the coast. Ben Bache, who was going with him, noted in his diary that all the people of Passy crowded around the litter to say goodbye. "A mournful silence reigned . . . only interrupted by a few sobs."

Franklin stopped for a few days at Southampton, to say goodbye to his English friends. There, he saw his son William for the last time. The meeting was not a friendly one. Franklin bought from William the farm he still owned in New Jersey, and gave it to William Temple. He presented William with a bill for 1,500 pounds—money that William owed him for Temple's education in England, and loans that Franklin had made to the Governor when they were trying to create the Ohio colony. William knew that if he had joined the Americans in the war, Franklin would have torn up these bills. Now, he was forced to give to his father the last land he owned in America—several thousand acres in upper New York State. Franklin also gave this land to Temple.

There was an additional reason why Franklin could not forgive William now. He was wanted for murder—the murder of a fellow American. Guerrilla raiders under his command had hanged in cold blood a captured American captain, Joshua Huddy. The Americans wanted to hang William in return, but he had jumped aboard a ship and gotten safely to England. So Franklin set sail for home, leaving his son behind him in England. William was paid a pension by the British government—750 pounds a year for the rest of his life.

To an English friend, who had worked to reconcile the two countries, Franklin was far more affectionate in his farewell. "We were long fellow laborers in the best of all works, the work of peace," he wrote. "I leave you still in the field, but having finished my day's work, I am going home to go to bed! Wish me a good night's rest, as I do you a pleasant evening. Adieu!"

CHAPTER 19

UNIFIER

ON THE TRIP HOME, FRANKLIN WROTE HIS LONG
delayed report on his study of the Gulf Stream. He told how
ships could shorten their passage from America to England by
as much as two weeks by using the three-mile-an-hour current of this great 10-mile-wide ocean river. By avoiding it on
the passage from Europe to America, they could save as much
as sixty or seventy miles a day. Modern scientists have not forgotten Franklin's discovery—the special submarine which
began exploring the Gulf Stream from top to bottom in 1969
was named the Benjamin Franklin.

Franklin said he was going home to bed, but he found there
was still work for him to do. The people of Pennsylvania
promptly elected him President of the Commonwealth, a job
that corresponds to the present-day governorship. Three
times he was reelected. It was, he told his sister Jane Mecom,

an honor he treasured more than a peerage, because it was the tribute of a free people.

The Continental Congress had not taken Franklin's advice when they passed their Articles of Confederation. As a central government for the thirteen colonies, Congress had no real power. Each state had one vote, which set small states and large states constantly bickering with each other. Relations between the states deteriorated alarmingly. They tended to ignore Congress almost completely, and act as if they were independent countries. They quarreled over their boundaries and began refusing to accept each other's money.

It was obvious that America needed a central government with more power to regulate disputes, organize the country, and pay off the large war debt. So Franklin was among the many Americans who welcomed the Constitutional Convention, when it met in Philadelphia in May, 1787. "Indeed if it does not do good, it must do harm," he told his successor in France, Thomas Jefferson, "as it will show that we have not wisdom enough among us to govern ourselves."

Franklin rallied all his strength in a last expression of commitment to the Cause. At the age of 82, for four consecutive months he trudged almost daily from his house to the Pennsylvania State House and spent hours wrangling and debating over how to reconcile poor states and rich states, large states and small states, slave states and free states. These were among the many questions confronted by the men who formulated the Constitution.

From the first day, Franklin sounded a call for a spirit of compromise. He could have asked for the job of chairman, but he deliberately stepped aside and allowed George Washington to be nominated without a contest. When the argument grew violent, Franklin warned the delegates that if they allowed themselves to be "divided by [their] little partial local interests," they would become "a reproach and a bye-word down to future ages."

Congress selected a "Grand Committee," consisting of one delegate from each state, to resolve the arguments between the large states and the small states. Franklin, picking up an idea that other men had already suggested, recommended that one house in Congress have equal representation, and the second house be represented in proportion to population. The committee agreed by a very narrow margin—5 to 4, with one state (Massachusetts) divided. Thus the Senate and the House of Representatives were created, thanks largely to Franklin's prestige and influence. This was a turning point in the Constitutional Convention. Once the small states felt their interests were protected, the Convention moved ahead with a minimum of argument.

As the Convention neared a close, however, another danger became apparent to the delegates. Many compromises had passed by a very close vote, and many of the losers in these votes were disgruntled and unreconciled. If a vote was taken on a man-by-man basis, it would reveal how many people did not like the Constitution as it now stood, even though a majority was in favor of it.

Franklin stepped forward to suggest one more great compromise. He urged everyone to sign the document as witnesses to the fact that all the *states* unanimously approved it. This was true—a majority on each state delegation did approve it. Franklin then went on to urge the delegates to support the Constitution in their separate states, when it was proposed for ratification. He admitted that he did not entirely approve the document at present. But in the course of his long life, he had changed his opinions on many important subjects. Perhaps his disagreements with the Constitution were wrong. He hoped that "every member of the Convention who may still have objections to it would with me on this occasion doubt a little of his own infallibility, and to make manifest our unanimity, put his name to this instrument." Franklin's proposal was carried, ten to nothing, and all but two of the delegates signed the Constitution.

Franklin, watching them walk up to the President's table to sign the historic document, pointed to a sun on the President's chair. "I have," he said, "often and often in the course of this session . . . looked at that . . . without being able to tell whether it was rising or setting: but now at length I have the happiness to know that it is a rising and not a setting sun."

Franklin lived two more years. His bladder stone grew

worse, and caused him terrible pain. But he seldom complained. He took deep pleasure in watching the successful
launching of the new American government. Writing to
George Washington soon after he became President, Franklin
congratulated him "on the growing strength of our new
government under your administration. For my own personal
ease, I should have died two years ago; but tho these years
have been spent in excruciating pain, I am pleased that I
have lived them, since they have brought me to see our present
situation."

At home, Franklin was surrounded by a warm and loving
circle. Sarah Bache and her seven children lived in the same
house with him. Widowed Polly Stevenson Hewson took his
advice and came over to America with her three children to be
near the man who was her spiritual father. She visited him
constantly, read to him and nursed him with tireless affection.

Only Temple Franklin worried his grandfather. He was
bored with country life, and neglected the New Jersey farm he
had inherited from his father. Franklin tried to win him an
American diplomatic appointment abroad, but Temple's reputation with his fellow Americans was not good. They considered him too much of a playboy. With all his grandfather's
influence behind him, he could not get the job he wanted.

In these last years, Franklin found time for one more cause.
He accepted the presidency of "The Pennsylvania Society for
Promoting the Abolition of Slavery, and the Relief of Free
Negroes Unlawfully Held in Bondage." In this capacity he

wrote sharp letters to the governors of many northern states, reproaching them for allowing their seamen, ship captains and merchants to participate in the slave trade. When the first Congress met, the Society presented a memorial, signed by Franklin, urging an immediate abolition of slavery. James Jackson of Georgia attacked the proposal, stating that slavery was sanctioned by the Bible and Negroes were better off and happier as slaves.

A few days later, an essay appeared in the *Federal Gazette,* Philadelphia's leading newspaper. It was supposed to be a statement by one Sidi Mehemet Ibrahim, a leading member of the Algerian government. Sidi argued against a small group of Algerians who wanted to abolish piracy and their country's nasty habit of enslaving white Christians. Sidi pointed out that Christians were far better off as slaves. They lived lives of perfect safety; they were well-fed, lodged and clothed. "They are not liable to be impressed for soldiers, and forced to cut one another's Christian throats, as in the wars of their own countries." The real writer, of course, was Franklin, ridiculing Jackson's speech in Congress. Although many Philadelphians were impressed, and Pennsylvania soon became one of the first northern states to abolish slavery, this terrible institution was too deeply entrenched in the southern states for Franklin or any other American of his time to defeat it.

A few weeks later, Franklin suffered an attack of pleurisy, the illness that had almost killed him when he was a young man of 21. This time, his old body was too worn out to resist it.

He slipped into a coma, and at 11 p.m. on April 17th, 1790, he died. He was 84.

The *Pennsylvania Gazette,* with a black border, announced his death. While bells tolled and 20,000 watched, his coffin was lowered into the grave in Christ Church burying ground, beside his wife, Deborah.

Scientists and statesmen around the world pronounced eulogies about his remarkable life. Perhaps the most moving tribute was spoken by the Comte de Mirabeau before the French National Assembly. The liberal nobleman declared that it was time for governments to mourn not only for kings, princes and generals, but for the benefactors of humanity. He called on the Assembly to join him "in a religious act" and wear mourning for three days to pay homage to this "mighty genius" who had freed men from the fear of both "thunderbolts and tyrants." The motion was passed by acclamation.

For many Americans, Franklin remains a puzzling man. Because he loved laughter and found humor in many things, some people have thought he was not serious about the things he believed in. Other people have dwelt on the advice he gave in his *Autobiography,* and in his almanacs, about how to save money and succeed at business. This is why Franklin's name appears so often on savings banks. These people have forgotten that Franklin quit making money at 42, and devoted the rest of his life to the study of science and service to his country.

Former President Harry S. Truman has said that Franklin "has not found his rightful place in American history yet." To some extent this is true. Perhaps it is time for us to follow Franklin's example, and learn to compromise the arguments we have among ourselves, and with the rest of the world. We can learn from him how to laugh and enjoy life, and still be serious about important things. Above all, if we follow his example, we will remain devoted to his ideal of America as a nation of free people.

Index

ABOUT THE AUTHOR

Noted author Thomas Fleming became interested in American history at the age of fourteen when he read *Oliver Wiswell* a novel about a loyalist in the American Revolution. Mr. Fleming has written more than a dozen books on the American Revolution including two much praised adult studies of Benjamin Franklin. *The New York Times* hailed *Benjamin Franklin, The Man Who Dared the Lightning* for "shedding new light" on Franklin.

Mr. Fleming's book *Liberty: The American Revolution* was a main selection of both the Book of the Month and History Book Clubs. Douglas Brinkley said it was "that rare essential book that belongs in every school and home." It was the companion volume to the prize-winning six part series of the same title that appeared on PBS.

Thomas Fleming appears frequently on PBS, the History Channel and C-Span as a commentator, Mr. Fleming lives in New York City with his wife, Alice, who is also a prolific author.

"Fleming has added new depth and vigor to a familiar subject of biographies. The facts that are usually glossed over in books for young readers, such as Franklin's penchant for dalliance, are given in a brisk and graceful style; there are many quotations from Franklin's writings and many anecdotes and bits of information not usually included in other books and giving evidence of thorough research. Above all, the vigor and informality of the writing make this a pleasure to read."

—ZENA SUTHERLAND, from *The Best in Children's Books*

BOOKS IN THIS SERIES

Admiral Richard Byrd: Alone in the Antarctic
BY PAUL RINK

Alexander the Great
BY JOHN GUNTHER

Amelia Earhart: Flying Solo
BY JOHN BURKE

The Barbary Pirates
BY C. S. FORESTER

Behind Enemy Lines: A Young Pilot's Story
BY H. R. DEMALLIE

Ben Franklin: Inventing America
BY THOMAS FLEMING

General George Patton: Old Blood and Guts
BY ALDEN HATCH

George Washington: Frontier Colonel
BY STERLING NORTH

Geronimo: Wolf of the Warpath
BY RALPH MOODY

Invasion: The Story of D-Day
BY BRUCE BLIVEN, JR.

John Paul Jones: The Pirate Patriot
BY ARMSTRONG SPERRY

Lawrence of Arabia
BY ALISTAIR MACLEAN

Path to the Pacific: The Story of Sacagawea
BY NETA LOHNES FRAZIER

The Sinking of the Bismarck: The Deadly Hunt
BY WILLIAM SHIRER

The Stouthearted Seven: Orphaned on the Oregon Trail
BY NETA LOHNES FRAZIER

Teddy Roosevelt: American Rough Rider
BY JOHN A. GARRATY

✷ STERLING POINT BOOKS